Life Skills for Autistic Teens

Nine essential tools for Adolescents on the Autism Spectrum to prepare them for independence

K. Davis-Reid

Introduction

Autism Spectrum Disorder (ASD) -More Than Meets The Eye

T hrough his theory of evolution, Charles Darwin was a scientist who forever changed biology and the way we see the world. Contrary to the popular image of an extroverted, flamboyant and witty genius that you have, Darwin barely talked to other people and mostly kept to himself.

Darwin was withdrawn, preferring to keep to his studies and experiments, both of which he was deeply immersed. He'd avoid communication with others and exchange information primarily through written notes instead of verbally. Does any of that sound familiar?

It's widely suspected that Charles Darwin and many other influential figures throughout history, Albert Einstein and

Steve Jobs, among many others, may have had autism based on the behavior they were exhibiting.

That can sound odd to a person whose child has Autism Spectrum Disorder, which can be defined as a neurological and developmental disorder that leads to impairments and defects in the brain's functioning and other secondary health complications. Looking at that definition, that's a lot of words with many negative connotations, right?

Being the parent or a caregiver for a child with autism can understandably make you focus on the condition as a description for deficits and impairments. You, better than anybody else, know the hardships and challenges all of you have endured. All the way from trying to explain what was different to your child, the endless medical consultations to finding the right professional treatment and adjusting everything about your life to accommodate.

It's a burden for both of you, and it's easy to see how in the face of so many obstacles, you can think of Autism Spectrum Disorder as an impairment that's serious enough to define your child. The condition exists on a spectrum, the more severe the symptoms are for your child, the more you associate your child with that label and warn others of their condition. As a worried parent, how can you not make sure to inform others of what they ought to be mindful of when it comes to your child?

Having ASD is a condition that affects every single aspect of a child's life, but it shouldn't be seen and treated as what defines them as people. Although autism is seen as a disorder where your child has "deficits" and "impairments," you probably know better than everyone else the charming personality, endearing quirks, staggering intelligence, and unmatched passion for hobbies and interests that your child can display.

Helping a child, as a parent, caregiver, or medical professional, begins with the recognition that ASD has a major influence over their life, but it's just one of many facets that they have. Each person, especially adolescents who are rapidly growing and blossoming as people in front of your eyes, is a complex and multi-layered combination of their passions, strengths, and the hardships they carry.

Acknowledging them as such is a vital first step to treating them better and increasing the effectiveness of any approach, whether behavioral or professional. The recognition of people with ASD as complex individuals not solely defined by their condition is especially important when it comes to the need for independence.

In many cases, there comes the point in time when individuals with ASD who have the opportunity have to learn how to manage on their own. Taking away the responsibility entirely or mostly from them is tiresome and not sustainable over the long term. It's also not beneficial for your child, as there is something deeply empowering to building the ability and confidence to live and thrive on their own.

ASD symptoms exist on a spectrum and intertwine very differently with the character, strengths, and circumstances of a person. Consequently, an individual with ASD will achieve different degrees of independence depending on the specific way in which their condition affects their life.

The journey towards self-sufficiency and independence can be arduous and full of obstacles and setbacks for you and the child. They are dependent and used to you always being by their side and providing assistance and guidance whenever necessary, while you are used to selflessly being by their side just in case. Teaching and helping them become more autonomous is a slow and gradual process, but the confidence and fulfillment it will bring to the child ultimately makes it worth it.

Who We Are

We are two parents who happen to have a child that's on the spectrum. Adjusting our lives to accommodate the needs of our son has been a challenging journey. Despite the exhaustion and frustration that must be more than familiar to you, too, we pulled through and want to share everything we learned along the way.

Raising a child on the spectrum and helping them reach independence to the degree that's feasible for them is a journey full of hardships and setbacks. It's a long-term effort that requires dedication, persistency, and perseverance when everything may seem hopeless.

Unlike the positive mantra that many resources encourage, we understand perfectly well why you can feel discouraged, frustrated, and even haunted by a sense of hopelessness when your best efforts don't give the desired result. This book serves as a guiding hand that will inspire you to stand back up and try again while giving you the actual practical tools you need to help your child reach independence.

What This Book Can Offer

The uncertainty and anxiety you feel over your child's future is not one that only you experience. Once your child enters the turbulent years of adolescence, they experience an urge for independence or uncertainty about what the future holds for them. Unprepared and looking with fear at the challenges ahead, they may doubt their ability to ever survive on their own. This book serves as a practical blueprint for forging an independent and empowered individual through the following steps:

- Chapter 1 - Describes the importance and types of personal care and how to achieve every aspect of personal care through the establishment of habits and routines.

- Chapter 2 - Describes the importance of communication for everyday success and the various systems and tools of communication you can employ to help your child.

- Chapter 3 - Describes the importance of social skills, recognizing the setbacks individuals with ASD may face and how to overcome them to improve the way they socialize with others.

- Chapter 4 - The importance of self-regulation and how to master your impulses and emotions for improved mental well-being.

- Chapter 5 - The importance of knowing your child's memory strengths and weaknesses and how to craft specific systems and exercises to compensate for challenges and take advantage of their natural talents.

- Chapter 6 - The importance of personal safety, how you can change the environment to prevent harmful and hazardous situations, and teaching your adolescent how to practice personal safety on their own.

- Chapter 7 - The often unrecognized importance of recreational skills, how to develop them in a manageable way and find joy, fulfillment, and purpose in those activities.

- Chapter 8 - The importance of personal finance for a stable and secure life and how individuals with ASD can learn the principles of personal finance for a more successful future.

- Chapter 9 - The importance of occupational skills and how to overcome employment challenges and utilize the strengths that ASD uniquely offers.

ASD is not an obstacle you simply overcome with the right type of behavior adjustments, routine changes, and system building. It's a life-long condition that offers unique challenges and obstacles to those who have it. This book serves as a bulletproof and thorough guide on managing the negative symptoms and taking full advantage of all strengths that your child has to propel them towards a more independent and better future.

Contents

Chapter One

Personal Care

P ersonal care keeps persons with ASD in an excellent physical and mental state allowing them to flourish and better interact with the world. The definition of personal care is a broad one and includes essential hygiene habits, eating and meal prep, strategies for organization and ways to improve mental health.

Helping a person with ASD develop personal care habits and routines is a significant first step towards independence as those habits are seen as essential for any person who wants to live or take care of themselves without outside assistance. Teaching personal care to a person with ASD can also be deeply empowering, giving them the confidence that they are capable on their own and showing them that if that's possible, then other steps towards independence are also very much achievable.

Why Do People With ASD Struggle With Personal Care?

People with ASD may struggle with personal care both for reasons related to their condition and out of behavioral habits that they came to adopt throughout their life.

One major issue people with ASD deal with is sensory overload. This is the uncomfortable and overwhelming feeling produced by being in touch with a certain object or while going through a specific experience. To you, the smell of the soap and deodorants may be appealing and generally an odor you've grown used to, while for a person with ASD, it can be immensely uncomfortable. The same goes for specific smells and textures in foods, the fabric of clothing, the noise from the hairdryer, the buzz of the microwave, and many other potential triggers.

Sensory overload isn't just some feeling that happens in certain situations and produces the same reaction. In some scenarios, the discomfort is present but manageable, while in others, people with ASD struggle immensely and it feels unbearable. The worse the experience with a specific object or event is, the more likely the person is to develop aversive behavior towards it. Doing an activity or following a routine can hardly be justified if it makes you feel uncomfortable and even if pushing through is an option, it's not a sustainable one over the long term.

Another issue with building personal care habits and routines can come from the struggle of people with ASD to understand the purpose and meaning behind a task. Although an issue is mostly seen in children with ASD, the struggle to grasp the importance of tasks is something many adolescents with the condition are also grappling with. Motivation and willingness to do a task can be very low if the activity does not produce a tangible change in the way they feel about themselves. It may be hard to visualize and understand what's the impact of regularly washing your hands, why three meals a day is essential, or why they need to have their hair cut once in a while.

Even with a purpose in mind, some activities are necessary but don't happen that frequently so developing tolerance and building the experience as a habit is an obstacle. Think of visits to medical professionals, visits to the dentist or even more minor tasks like cleaning up your room and having your hair cut. When the occasion happens once in a while, a person with ASD may forget altogether, too caught up in their passions and other activities, or the tolerance they had developed may be reduced because it's been a while since the last occasion.

Seeing medical professionals and the dentist can especially be an issue for those with ASD. Even if there is an established frequency with regular checkups that are known and expected, there is much room to feel overwhelmed and anxious from such a visit. Sensory overload is possible in a busy medical facility or in the cabinet of a medical professional with the potent smell of medicine and the beaming lights that illuminate the whole room. It's uncomfortable and very stressful to wait in line, wondering what you will be told by the medical professional or fearing that they will say that something is wrong with you. Even if you can in some way see the reason behind everything, the anxiety that tightens your chest is hard to overcome.

Visits to a medical professional can very often feel like an intrusion of privacy as well which can lead to lots of anxiety and aversive behavior towards those essential visits. Having to explain your behavior, how you are feeling, and what you are thinking to a medical professional can feel like a personal interrogation for people with ASD. There can also be an issue of physical distance, being at the dentist requires somebody in very close proximity to you who will be operating inside your mouth, which is a very sensitive area and also a space that's considered very personal for people.

The final issue has to do with learned dependency. Personal care routines and habits are essential for the health and well-being of an adolescent with ASD, so if they naturally struggle to deal with them, it's easy to see why parents would step in to help them. Assistance for personal care can continue for a while past the point where a child can begin to take care of themselves. Maybe the activity is unpleasant, and they don't find the purpose in it, so an external push is required. Perhaps the parent or caretaker is anxious if the child will manage on their own and in a busy household, it's better to choose the secure and safe option by helping them once again.

With time, children who have very little experience and understanding of the task begin to prefer and expect somebody else to do those activities with them. A person with ASD may be especially averse to change due to their condition. Very often, changes in routine or the introduction of new experiences and requirements, especially unpleasant ones, don't receive a positive reaction and willingness to cooperate. The inflexible behavior can be a serious obstacle in assisting the child towards a better personal care routine and system.

Giving an in-depth explanation of why children with ASD struggle with personal care is essential for you to understand the root cause of the issue. Assistance and efforts to change behavior and build beneficial habits as we keep those unique challenges in mind and seek ways to overcome them in a manner that's gradual and manageable for the child.

How To Practice Personal Care

Teaching a child with ASD how to practice personal care is a slow and gradual process. The effort towards better personal care requires you to keep in mind the unique challenges they are facing and how they can slow down or, at times, even lead to regressions. It's about proactively creating an environment and changing their mindset and motivations in a way that makes them accepting of the change.

Personal Hygiene

Improving personal hygiene begins with a friendly but very clear explanation of the importance of personal hygiene for the health and social experiences of a child with ASD. Very often, habits and actions that feel bothersome or outright unpleasant can hardly be connected to having any purpose when it feels like torture just for the sake of torture. You have to explain to them why they have important health and social implications so that the expected behavior has an actual meaning when they think of it.

It's often helpful to connect the behavior you expect from them with some desire or goal that they already have. For example, showering regularly, brushing your teeth, and combing your hair are important to be perceived positively by those around you. This gives you the opportunity to form relationships better and discuss your passions and interests with other people. Brushing your teeth and eating regularly can be tied to the desire to be healthy. Who wouldn't want to feel physically and mentally well and avoid uncomfortable visits to the doctor or dentist?

Another obstacle related to personal hygiene has to do with sensory overload. Taking a shower can be a whole challenge on its own, the different temperatures of the water, the potent smell of the soap and shampoo, and the irritating sensation of the sponge against your skin can all feel uncomfortable and even overwhelming. If you are sensitive, then the torture continues when you ought to brush your teeth and feel an unpleasant aroma in your mouth for two minutes and then have it linger in your mouth afterward. Deodorants, hairdryers, and anything else that follows, the hardships can seem endless for a person with ASD.

Making personal care feels less unpleasant starts with the observation of which activities the child does not enjoy in particular and asking them what's uncomfortable and overwhelming about them. If it's the feeling of warm water gradually hitting their skin then, then having a bath may be a better idea than a shower. If it's the unpleasant smell of soap, shampoo, or toothpaste, then you can consider alternatives that don't produce the same reaction. It's important to be alert about what they enjoy and what they tend to avoid and recognize that they are facing unique challenges that need to be acknowledged and addressed.

How successful a personal hygiene routine is also depends on how they generally feel about being clean. Some children with ASD generally dislike the sensation of being clean, while others adore it, but they just hate the process of getting there. For those that enjoy the feeling of being clean, it may be helpful to remind them and make them visualize how pleasant and comfortable feeling clean would be as a way to motivate them to push through the discomfort and get to that state.

For children that don't enjoy the sensation altogether and feel uncomfortable through and through, you can work on minimizing the discomfort and establishing it as a necessity that they naturally learn to do. Making sure you reduce discomfort can happen by changing the products and tools, say using an electric toothbrush instead of a regular one, and it can also happen by breaking the routine into smaller bits when possible. For example, brushing your teeth in the morning and washing your hands and face can happen sometime before taking a shower. Setting a distance between what ought to be done means that the child with ASD can avoid the overwhelming feeling that all those activities can produce if combined together.

Those separate tips and tricks can be useful as assistance at the beginning of the journey and as tools to keep in mind, but the biggest challenge comes with the need to make personal hygiene part of your child's routine. On one hand, including uncomfortable and bothersome activities with no assistance into the routine of a person with ASD can be a frustrating experience and feel nearly impossible. On the other hand, once you successfully craft a routine that's manageable and sustainable, then the rigidness and consistency that it establishes mean that the child will likely stick with it.

Developing habits and routines is a gradual process, if a child is used to receiving assistance, then suddenly plunging them into the unknown with high expectations is counter-productive and may make them less willing to try in the future. The process begins by picking a habit, such as brushing your teeth and trying to build it as part of your routine. Doing that successfully means having them do the activity at a comfortable time when they can continue to make the same habit every day. For some, brushing their teeth happens instantly after they wake up, while for others, it happens after lingering in bed for a while, stretching, and preparing for the day ahead first. It's all about picking a time that's comfortable and sustainable over the long term because the whole point is to make the process automatic.

Making a habit part of an essential hygiene routine shouldn't just be like pushing a boulder on a hill, enduring the suffering until you just get used to it. There are ways for you to make the process more fun and interesting. For example, attaching a habit tracker on the wall or installing an application where you can keep track of how long the activity has been done every single day. Brushing your teeth every day for two weeks could become an obstacle that you ought to overcome and a milestone for which you will receive a reward.

Getting a reward can be a very effective way to promote healthy behavior when an activity initially isn't very enjoyable. It's important to think of small rewards that you can give to a person who's doing their best to improve their personal care. Even something as little as a comment of appreciation and admiration for their efforts can go a long way in validating their feelings and motivating them to continue improving.

Sometimes a struggle to develop a habit and maintain a routine can happen out of forgetfulness and disorganization. Having cues around the house that remind the child with ASD that they ought to do a certain activity, such as a colorful illustration with essential habits for the morning attached to a wall, can be a very effective way to assist with that. Using timers, reminders, and setting an automatic digital system that reminds the need to do a task at a specific point in time can also be beneficial since getting caught up in homework, hobbies, or other passions can make somebody with ASD forget that there are habits they ought to go through for the day.

Getting Used To Medical Professionals

Sensory overload, fear of the unknown, and the inability to understand the meaning behind medical visits can pose serious challenges for a person with ASD.

It may seem obvious to many but hard to conceptualize for a person with ASD what's the purpose behind checkups and frequent medical visits, especially when they often feel overwhelmed with anxiety, fear, and uncertainty over what may follow. Overcoming this hardship begins by explaining clearly why they are necessary and how they are very beneficial. Medical checkups aren't random questions you ought to periodically answer, but a way to make sure everything is going well and problems can be addressed early on. Going to the dentist to fix a cavity is one way to prevent an issue that would grow worse over time and avoid future pain.

Since people with ASD enjoy sticking to a routine that gives them certainty, it's important to be transparent and very clear about when medical checkups and appointments are coming up on the calendar in a way that's visible to them. They not only know it's coming, but it helps them to better process the idea so that they are better prepared.

When you visit the doctor or dentist's office, you can reduce the anxiety and discomfort by picking an appointment that minimizes waiting time, for example, at the beginning or the end of the working day. You can also take them to the place one or two times before the actual appointment so they can grow more familiar with the place and the environment if a sensory overload is an issue, you can find a quiet place to wait outside of the usual buzz and bring distractions and comforters to keep them from growing too anxious.

It's especially helpful if you pick a medical professional and a dentist over the long term, and they happen to be somebody who understands the hardships the child may be facing. Dealing with medical visits is much less frightening when you have a professional on the other side that wants to minimize anxiety.

Diet & Meal Prepping

A good nutritional diet can be challenging for a person with ASD. Sensory overload can be the taste, smell, and texture of a certain food that can make it unbearable or ruin a whole meal. A person with ASD may have certain conditions that do not allow them to eat properly, they may prefer to eat somewhere quiet with no noise, or they are only comfortable eating in the company of people they know, sometimes they prefer to be by themselves when eating. Over-fixations and obsessions with certain foods can lead to an unhealthy and unbalanced diet too.

Sensitivity to certain textures is an issue many children with ASD encounter, they may enjoy the taste and smell, but the food's still hard to swallow. When sensory overload from foods is an issue, you can consider alternatives that don't produce the same results. If the foods the child is avoiding are healthy and essential such as fruits and veggies, then you can try to cook and present them in a different way. For example, blending and smoothing veggies in dishes and soups means that you can avoid the uncomfortable soggy texture. If raw fruits are an issue because of the sinewy texture, then you can consider smoothies or yogurts that contain some fruits as an alternative. If the issue comes down to taste, then you can try different recipes of veggies, fruits, and other healthy foods you want to include in the diet or add them to ones they enjoy, such as pizza and vegetable sticks with their favorite dip, burritos, etc.

Over-eating and under-eating can both be problems that children with ASD experience. Over-eating can be treated by reducing portions and limiting the time when food and snacks can be consumed. If over-eating, especially with snacks, is a persistent issue, you can consider restricting access. However, the most effective long-term strategy is to give them a clear explanation of why excessive snacking is not healthy and to help them find ways and reasons to limit snacking. For example, many people voluntarily reduce the snacks they consume by not buying any, not having them be visible in the house, or using them only as a reward when their other goals such as work for the day or having two healthy meals have been completed.

On the other hand, under-eating can be an issue for multiple reasons. One explanation is that the food isn't appealing or something in the way one unpleasant food is combined with the other they enjoy or there's a combining of foods, to begin with, that discourages eating. Sometimes the issue is the environment, wherein in a certain setting and context with certain people, the child consumes less than usual. For both those issues, you need to carefully observe their reaction to what's presented and try to pinpoint the specific cause of discomfort so the necessary changes can be made accordingly. Just as with over-eating, helping them eat the right amount is a huge help, but there's also a need to gradually teach them and observe their behavior better, what makes them feel uncomfortable and reduces their desire to eat and to try to make the necessary corrections.

Independence when it comes to nutrition comes down to practice, you should actively let them participate and encourage them to be involved in the food-making process. This way, they can learn cooking basics and some recipes, and it sparks interest and curiosity to discover more on their own.

People with ASD enjoy having certainty and a strict routine, so automating the process of cooking and meal preparing can be greatly beneficial. Whether it's colorful sticky notes with their favorite recipes or using cooking applications with them and giving the instructions for cooking the meals, making cooking as convenient as possible can be a great benefit.

Furthermore, the routine can also be interpreted as eating at approximately the same time every day, which can be immensely helpful in ensuring that a person with ASD doesn't get too caught up in work, hobbies, or anything else and forgets to have a meal.

Sometimes there's too much going on, so buying groceries and preparing food in bulk can mean no meal is ever skipped, especially if the person enjoys having similar or the same meals multiple times throughout the week, so they don't mind the similarity. When there's no time to cook and prepare anything, snacks that you have stashed around can be a great way to reduce hunger pangs and give yourself a boost of energy.

Mental Health

The discourse around personal care is dominated by hygiene routines, organization of your room and environment, and eating regularly. While those are all essential and healthy lifestyle choices that each person should practice, an often neglected aspect of personal care is the need for us to have a healthy relationship with ourselves and our emotions.

Being a person with ASD can be a mentally exhausting and emotionally draining experience. Struggling with communication, building relationships with others, and facing stigmatization, dismissal, and lack of understanding from society can feel soul-crushing. It can make you feel inferior and reduce your self-worth and confidence significantly. Experiencing such unique challenges makes it easy to see why a person with ASD may feel crowded with negative thoughts about the world and themselves.

Mental health struggles can be especially challenging in early adolescence when a person is growing up, trying to figure out who they are and what they want out of life.

Being the parent or caretaker of a person with ASD places you in a tricky situation where you should give emotional support to the child while also making sure to give them room to breathe, express, and figure out their emotions. Adolescence is a time when children feel a sudden urge for independence, especially so when they were previously very reliant on their parents, and they see how friends around them are also seeking to be more autonomous. This is why giving advice, trying to uplift their spirits, and validating them should be done more gently so as not to intrude on their personal space, and you should make it very clear that you are always there to comfort them and listen to what they have to say.

Lifting their spirits and encouraging them isn't just the compliments that you give them daily. It's the continuous effort to show a person with ASD that they are wonderful, and their condition does not define who they are in spite of being a considerable influence over their life. It's about gently but firmly showing them the unique strengths and skills that they possess in order to validate how they feel and help them develop those advantages. Facing hardships and rejection from your social circles while being uncertain about the future can make a person very pessimistic about their self-perception, this is why it's important to often remind them of their worth and teach them to recognize their immense value as an individual.

As a parent or caretaker of somebody with ASD, you know very well, that the world isn't always butterflies and rainbows. Sometimes you can't help but feel exasperated, angry, and sad about the way something is going in your life. This is why a healthy approach toward mental health tries to uplift the spirits of somebody by making them recognize the positives they experience and their self-worth while not stifling any negative emotions that are brewing inside of them.

It's about practicing seeing, recognizing, and accepting the feelings that you are experiencing, even if they are not pleasant or comfortable. Trying to shove them inside yourself only worsens how you psychologically feel and does not mean that eventually, they won't break free in a much harsher way towards somebody or yourself. When you see a person with ASD displaying signs of emotional turmoil and sadness, it's vital to gently suggest that they express what they are feeling to you or to a therapist and medical professional.

Putting your emotions in words can help you get them out of your system and better understand what you are going through as you try to describe it.

Expression of emotions is important. Many people with ASD prefer keeping to themselves with certain issues, especially when they feel uncomfortable, uncertain, or anxious about their feelings. When talking to their parents, caretaker, or therapist is not an option, then they can practice individual ways to express their emotions and thoughts.

One convenient way to do so is journaling. Whether on a piece of paper or digitally on a document, journaling and writing down your thoughts doesn't need to have a rigid structure. It's about recognizing the emotions you have pent up and pouring them out somewhere instead of trying to deny them or hiding in shame for what you are going through. There's no right or wrong way to journal and write down your thoughts, it can be done every single day as a habit, from time to time when you need it, on voice messages where you verbally pour out all your woes or on a document where you write with caps to express your anger.

Journaling can be very therapeutic, cathartic, and an effective tool for self-discovery. Growing more comfortable with your emotions and expressing them also means that a person with ASD is more likely to open up to others about their issues once confrontation with their feelings is not that intimidating.

Improving your mental health is also about discovering more about yourself as a person, pursuing your interests and passions, and allowing yourself to take breaks. People with ASD can develop an unhealthy balance between work and responsibilities, and time off. A low sense of self-worth and confidence, along with stigmatization from those around them, can push a person with ASD to seek perfect grades in school and work on extracurriculars and outside projects as a way to compensate for some failing they believe they have. A tendency to forget about their surroundings and hyper-focus on a project can also contribute to neglect for themselves, other people, and responsibilities outside of what they are currently doing.

Studying and working too much without sufficient breaks can lead to mental exhaustion and burnout, which is why a healthy balance between work and rest ought to be established and taught from an early age. Everybody needs to rest and take time off, especially adolescents who have a lower capacity to work as much and people with ASD whose sensory overload and obstacles with emotional dysregulation can lead to faster burnout.

Scheduling demanding hobbies, extracurriculars, and projects along with mandatory breaks can be an effective way to set boundaries. Furthermore, many people use alarms that signal to them when the "workday" is over so that any studying remaining will be left for the next day. Reminders from parents and caregivers to take breaks and time off can be immensely helpful as an accountability check when forgetfulness and the irrational urge to keep working may otherwise dominate.

A final note has to be made about pursuing passions, interests, and hobbies. Finding meaning and fulfillment in life often comes through creativity, where a person can chase what they love and express themselves. Unfortunately, there's often stigmatization of interests and passions that people may have, with many deeming them "silly," "stupid," "useless," and reducing them to obsessions. It's important to counter such dismissive and judgemental claims whenever given the opportunity and remind people with ASD who have their own interests that there's nothing wrong or shameful about what they love. Diving deep into a topic, being a walking encyclopedia on a very specific subject, and having the passion for talking for hours on that matter is something that they should not feel regret and guilt for doing.

Personal care is one of the most essential lists of habits, routines, and systems of behavior that a person with ASD ought to develop as a way to propel themselves towards higher independence and confidence. As a parent and caretaker, it's important to recognize what are the unique challenges they go through, address them and gradually teach them how to spot and resolve those issues by themselves.

Chapter Two

Communication

C ommunication is one of the most essential skills for a person who wants to effectively and meaningfully interact with the world. Banter with friends and relatives, making a public speech in front of an audience, or communicating with your manager at work, each of those experiences requires proper communication skills.

Teens on the spectrum experience various difficulties communicating with others and may rely on other unconventional forms of communication. Contrary to popular belief, communication is like any other skill that can be taught and mastered through proper professional and personal guidance.

Why Teens With ASD Struggle With Communication

Many people take communication as a given, either you can communicate with others or you can't. In truth, communication requires many small skills for it to be effective, with each of them capable of being taught individually. In its most abstract form, communication is the ability to quickly shift your attention and retain it from a person offering you information, listening carefully, and formulating an appropriate response for the situation.

Seeing communication this way makes it seem more complicated than initially anticipated. One must concentrate on what others are saying, respond appropriately based on the verbal message given and visual cues, and self-monitor themselves throughout the whole conversation. People with ASD may struggle with each of those steps or may experience significant hardships with one of them in particular.

For example, concentration may be disrupted if a person with ASD zones out, bounces from one topic to another, or hyper-focuses on one topic of discussion in particular while ignoring the rest. Responding appropriately may not happen if a person with ASD fails to read the meaning behind a person's word because often, people on the spectrum struggle with idiomatic language, sarcasm, irony, and metaphors in general. Finally, conversations require quick replies, so a person with ASD may struggle to read all visual cues in time and make the appropriate judgment over how the other person is feeling right now.

Communication issues can also be related to the way people are used to conventional forms of communication. If verbal communication is unsuccessful, children with ASD turn towards gestures, emotionally charged sounds, pictures, or even directly guide you towards what they are trying to say. Such alternative forms of communication may result from a struggle to express themselves verbally. Adolescents with ASD often struggle to formulate sentences because they confuse pronouns, repeat words over and over and turn to echolalia. One example, in particular, is echolalia which is when a person may repeat phrases that seem out of context but are actually related to something they've heard or watched elsewhere. Such phrases may not perfectly fit, but, nevertheless, they describe a concrete thought or emotion that the child is going through. Very often, those phrases are taken from one person, from movies or television programs where they may be continuously repeated.

One final issue with communication worth mentioning is the environment in which people on the spectrum are trying to communicate with others. It's preferable to be with people and in an environment in which they feel safe and comfortable. Even if that's not possible, people with ASD need to be taught how to manage foreign and stressful environments as there's only so much you can do to reduce them.

Only through understanding the root issues that people on the spectrum are facing can we develop a system and methodology to address them properly.

The Importance Of a Growth Mindset

Becoming better at anything comes with a firm belief that you have the ability to improve. Many people get stuck with a fixed mindset over their ability to improve. Some think their intelligence is fixed from birth, others believe that if they are socially awkward and struggle with conversations, then this is just a curse they will struggle with for the rest of their life.

The myth of fixed abilities is especially prevalent when it comes to communication and any other social skill. People tend to believe that if you are an engaging speaker, humorous presenter, or generally able to encourage interesting conversations, then it's a natural gift. You must have been born as this interesting, charismatic, and smooth-talking person. This couldn't be farther from the truth. Even if you are naturally inclined to perform better in those skills, that doesn't mean that a person who struggles in the beginning, doesn't have the ability to improve significantly.

A belief in your worth as an individual and your ability to improve yourself is the foundation for any positive and meaningful change. A person who does not have faith in themselves may be exposed to the best professionals, a supportive social network, and know the most effective systems for improvement in a field, but they'd all be futile if the belief in yourself isn't present. What's the point of making an effort continuously or being receptive to feedback if there's little to no chance of progress?

As a caretaker or a parent, teaching a person with ASD that they have the ability to become better at communication is crucial for any strategy to work. Making a person believe they can become better begins with the acknowledgment that not everything is sunlight and rainbows at the moment. People on the spectrum likely, to varying degrees, experience problems communicating, and the consequences are often guilt, shame, and social exclusion. It's vital to acknowledge the hardships they've gone through and give them a sense of hope for a better future, not just promise them that it will get better while ignoring just how much they may be struggling right now.

Embracing a growth mindset for communication and social skills may be especially difficult due to the unique stigma against improving your social skills. If people falsely believe that your natural communicative abilities are there to stay, then an effort for improvement feels artificial or even wrong. You must have seen the critiques and mockery of some insensitive people who equate improving your communication abilities to "teaching a robot how to be human" or "showing a self-learning AI what emotions are."

If a child with ASD is exposed to such remarks or similar types of stigmatization, then it's important to dismiss them by thoroughly explaining how they are uncalled for, not helpful, and outright false. If that's not effective, for some children embracing such remarks but spinning them into a positive can be very empowering. For example, the comparison to a robot or anything else can be turned into an amusing metaphor where they "upgrade" themselves to be better and stronger.

What Even Is a Good Conversation?

Knowing what you are striving towards is important for all persons, especially those on the spectrum who tend to take instructions and guidance literally and need a lot of clarity on what's expected and required from them. It's probably easy to see how telling a person to "open up," "stop talking from time to time," or just "become a better conversation partner" is vague and unhelpful in encouraging or guiding them in the right direction for improvement.

A good conversation is one that flows naturally, where two people smoothly transition from one talking to the other, and they feel comfortable and secure in expressing themselves. There are many ways for you to illustrate that concept to a person with ASD. For example, think of throwing a ball with somebody else, it's fun when the ball keeps getting tossed from one person to the other, and this smooth back and forth is done in a way so that the other person can actually catch the ball and doesn't get hit by it, making them uncomfortable.

Another way to think of it can be if two people are doing a presentation together, each of them has a unique perspective and information towards a mutual goal that they wish to share, trusting the other person and letting them take some of that responsibility with you leads to the best result, instead of trying to do everything yourself and ignoring what the other person can add.

Daniel Wendler, an author on the spectrum who's dedicated his life to improving the social skills of others, speaks of "inspiration" and "invitation" as the key ingredients for a smooth, comfortable and meaningful conversation. Inspirations would be the way you make another person comfortable and willing to express themselves with no inhibitions. Invitations would be the remarks and cues you give, which make it clear to a conversation partner that it's their turn to speak. Following that should help make a conversation flow well and minimize all the uncomfortable pauses and awkward segues.

Invitations would be the more direct tool for starting a conversation and keeping up a conversation with a stranger or somebody you don't know very well. It involves directly asking them a question about a recent experience they may have had, what they are up to these days, or asking their opinion on a mutual interest you both have. The rule of thumb when asking questions is to make them open and have room for sharing and interpretation, so the person on the other side is encouraged to share more than just a yes or no answer.

Invitations are an excellent ice breaker and can serve as a segue towards a different topic but inspiring the other person is where the smoothness and flow of a conversation really come through. To inspire a person to share is a more subtle and challenging task because it involves them getting much more comfortable talking with you and being willing to share personal matters. Engaging a conversation partner in such a way is easier if you two know each other, but it can also happen with total strangers.

Inspiring a person to share begins with a comfortable environment in which you show a genuine interest in their experiences and them as an individual. People feel comfortable and secure when they are given an adequate opportunity to express themselves and feel as though they are actively being listened to and not interrupted. Comfort can also be maintained when a person learns to avoid uncomfortable topics and sticks to what the person on the other side enjoys based on the visual or verbal cues they may provide. Finally, inspiring another person to share is a two-way effort, a person is more likely to share if you appear comfortable, honest, and even a bit vulnerable while sharing your experiences.

With both invitations and inspirations, it's vital to pick the most suitable topics throughout the conversation. Excellent topics are usually ones related to something both people are going through and are close to the current social context. If you are in class, it makes sense to ask a classmate how they are feeling about the upcoming test.

Depending on how you ask, a topic can provide for a very different interpretation and conversation. For example, if somebody shares about a hobby they have, such as swimming, you can both ask where they swim or how often, and you can also ask what made them start swimming or what keeps them going. As you can probably guess, the second one is much more engaging because it encourages the person to think and share their unique preferences and experiences. While asking them how often they swim will make you learn a fact about their world, asking them how they started can give a story on how they were inspired by their father, who's a competitive swimmer, or how the feeling of being in the pool keeps them going.

No topic is universally interesting or engaging for all people, which is why it's important to keep that in mind while having a conversation with somebody else. While in the following chapter, we will explore in-depth the nuances in body language that signal when a person's interested or not, for now, it's important to note that abrupt changes in behavior are usually a signal that a topic should be halted or avoided altogether. If a person was cheerful and laughing at one point, but their replies grew shorter and stiffer once a topic continued to be discussed more in-depth or another one was brought up, then it's time to segue towards a different topic.

Strategies For Improving Communication Skills

Improving communication skills is far from an easy journey, it's full of hardships and setbacks, and progress won't always be visible. Encouraging and guiding a person to improve how they communicate with others requires both the parent or caretaker and the person with ASD to truly understand that it's a gradual process. It sounds so obvious that you'd think it's unnecessary to mention, but progress does not happen at the same rate compared to other activities.

Think of a person on the spectrum who picks up a new hobby like chess, they begin to constantly play, practice, and watch resources on variations. With more experience, they begin to notice patterns, and the whole process gradually becomes more automated while the intentional moves they play are guided by their gradually developed expertise. Improving communication skills works in a similar way, but a person may struggle more and experience more obstacles because social interactions are not something you can always control no matter how hard you try, and handling a conversation has many complex factors that ought to be mastered.

Saying that improvement of communication skills is hard does not mean it's impossible, quite the opposite even. Nevertheless, it's necessary to acknowledge that the road ahead may be bumpy or obscured from time to time because excessively high expectations and intolerance to a lack of progress can lead to a lack of motivation, burnout, and giving up altogether.

How small and gradual the next step depends entirely on how impaired communication is with that specific individual and the guidance and suggestions offered by the professionals you are working with. For somebody with severe impairments in communication, teaching them to say the specific word corresponding to what they want as compared to using phrases or pointing towards the item or food they want is a huge victory. For somebody else who's learning to hold conversations on their own but struggles with keeping up, you can practice slowing down, using slang and informal language that they are comfortable with, or just shortening the sentences altogether.

Not everyone begins from the same starting point, so it's essential to be mindful of that and approach learning and practice with patience. Allowing a person with ASD to practice talking even with shorter sentences, more time between responses, or more time to say what they mean multiple times is an effective way to gradually give them room to improve. Before you know it, they will start to get better and require less assistance or compromises on behalf of the person they are speaking with.

When it comes to expressing what they want and following orders, people with ASD have a distaste for ambiguity. Saying that they should get ready for school or help with dinner can be vague and leave them uncertain about what exactly is expected of them, so you should make sure to specify exactly what's expected of them. Effective and clear communication can be established between the parent or caretaker and the child, but they must also learn to manage on their own. This is why it's important to gradually teach them what certain phrases or responsibilities, even if sounding vague, may expect from them and to have them practice asking politely and gently for specific instructions if the task remains unclear.

Effective communication can also be fostered based on the communities in which they participate and the environment in which they are interacting with others. If it's relaxing, fun, and enjoyable, then they are more likely to open up to others, be less anxious and uptight about potential mistakes and make more attempts to talk with people even if initially they face obstacles. As they are growing up, the parent or caretaker can make sure to introduce them to environments and communities that would accept them and be mindful of any accommodations that ought to be made. With time, a person with ASD will have more freedom and will have to learn how to introduce themselves and inform others of the way their communication may be different compared to others.

When it comes to informing others of your condition, it doesn't have to be in a negative and self-deprecating way, saying that you face some struggles but are doing your best to improve and would love for others to have a bit more patience is an equally effective and much more helpful way to look at the situation.

Although self-regulation will be explored thoroughly in Chapter 4, it's important to briefly note its important purpose when communicating with others. Whether you should speak on a topic or continue diving deep into one depends on the reaction of the person you are talking to. One should always be mindful if a person's voice grows stiff, their responses shorten, or their body language becomes defensive, as that's a sign they don't enjoy the direction in which the conversation is going.

Self-monitoring can also be important when the room should be given for another person to speak or ask a question during the conversation. People with ASD have many passions and interests, and asking them about their experiences and what they enjoy can make them hyper-fixate on saying every single possible detail. One way to stop yourself and to make sure the interaction is enjoyable for both is to think of the answer you give as a puzzle full of many pieces. If somebody asks how your current hobby is going, you can probably talk for hours, giving them the whole puzzle at once. You can also put down 2-3 pieces of that puzzle by sharing some of your recent experiences and then giving them room to reply and see if they are interested in learning more.

If a person on the spectrum struggles with self-monitoring, one effective way to handle that is to make listening to others a habit. If conversations are a roughly 50/50 separation of who's going to be talking, then allowing and encouraging the other person to share how they are feeling and what they are thinking can be an effective way to stop oneself from going on tangents and be more selective in your replies.

All those skills and techniques can be gradually taught to a person on the spectrum in a comfortable and safe environment, but they are not the only available options. There are groups and professionals who specialize in intentionally creating programs and environments where people can learn those skills from the ground up. Communication issues and remedies can be explored in therapy or group therapy, while communication and other related social skills can be taught in social skills training camps, high school or college classes on acting, speaking, and communication. Having regular practice in a safe environment with many experienced people to supervise the process can be of great benefit towards the steady improvement of communication skills.

Therapy and counseling can be of great assistance when communication issues stem from social anxiety, low confidence, or other issues that ought to be resolved prior to or simultaneously with the effort to communicate better.

Practice and Setting Goals

Assistance from parents and caregivers as well as professionals in various fields related to communication can be a significant help, but over the long term, a person with ASD who's determined to improve ought to practice on their own to maintain and improve their abilities.

Communication with others is just like any other skill that you can think of. Consistency, daily practice, and resilience in the face of challenges will lead to exponential improvement and tangible results over time. When somebody says, you ought to be consistent, many associate this with the need to always go above and beyond and work hard to improve. The truth is that some days we are understandably busy with other tasks and responsibilities, while on others, we are too physically or mentally exhausted to have time or energy to give towards improvement.

Keeping that in mind, consistency would mean trying to do something every day to practice, even if for a few minutes, and forgiving yourself when the ability to do anything just isn't there. After all, having a mindset for consistent improvement means long-term progress, which is not linear, nor does it exclude taking breaks from time to time as long as you get back to it eventually.

Practicing communication means assessing your flaws and figuring out which exercises and drills will be of benefit to improve. Figuring this out should initially be done with the assistance of parents, caregivers, and professionals, but gradually the person with ASD should be encouraged to also reflect on what they struggle with and what ought to be improved. Knowing what's the exact issue and which exercises are effective in improving it is a process of trial and error. Listening to audiobooks and reading books to increase your vocabulary, discussing hobbies and passions with a friend, enrolling in hobbies related to public speaking, going to social events, and making an intentional effort to start conversations, are just some of the many ways in which a person on the spectrum can try to improve their communication skills.

One additional option when it comes to practice is to set up short and long-term goals. Knowing precisely what you want to improve upon can be very effective in helping you set up the right exercises and channel your focus on certain activities in order to reach that goal. If you happen to have a short-term goal of learning how to approach and begin conversations with strangers and a long-term goal of having a whole conversation in which the other person is comfortable and engaged, then the progress can be tracked to see how well you are doing.

Experimentation versus Comfort

Life is about learning more about yourself, strengths, weaknesses, preferences, and interests. One of the most natural and effective ways to do that is through meaningfully communicating with other people, especially in situations where you don't know everything that may happen. No matter how much you put in the effort, inevitably, mistakes will continue to happen. Keeping that in mind, it's important to help people with ASD who want to improve their communication skills to avoid perfectionism and embrace failure whenever it happens.

Many people frame failure as this horrible experience where you feel ashamed and horrible for making a mistake. A more positive and helpful way to think of failures and mistakes is to assume they are natural and acceptable, everybody makes them, and it's actually beneficial that they happen since each one holds an important lesson that you ought to remember in the future. Mistakes are acceptable and shouldn't be avoided, but if certain types of behaviors are not only wrong but have actively hurt another person and how they feel, a sincere apology is due.

Experimentation should be encouraged, but that shouldn't stigmatize ways in which people with ASD over time realize that they'd prefer to communicate. There's no single right way to communicate with people, and those on the spectrum should be given the freedom to settle and opt-in for ways that make them feel most comfortable and capable of communicating. For example, many have found that texting allows them more time to compose themselves and better express their thoughts. On the contrary, others prefer voice calls and talking with others verbally because they can better read their tone and receive visual cues on how they are feeling.

There's no right or wrong way to improve your communication skills, but it's essential that adolescents with ASD receive personal and professional assistance and guidance while also being taught how to improve on their own in the future.

Communication skills as with anything else in life are not a fixed ability nor should they be perceived as such. Even if a person has a different starting point, they still have the potential to significantly improve their communication skills.

Chapter Three

Social skills

- -

While communicating relates specifically to how a person shares information with another, social skills are an umbrella term for anything involving verbal and non-verbal communication and expressions that we use to interact with people daily.

Just as with communication, social skills are a field in which people with ASD often struggle with. While neurotypical people may find social skills and interactions intuitive and easy to learn, those on the spectrum find it much more difficult to learn social skills and require intentional effort and supervision to master them.

While the difficulty may be harder, it's important to stress the fact that every person has the ability to improve their social skills, and they are not doomed to stay at the same level no matter how much they try.

Assessing Strengths and Weaknesses

If it's possible, in many cases, it's best to work with therapists, counselors, and social skills professionals to assess what a person with ASD is struggling with and what ought to be done to provide improvement to their social skills.

Professional practice usually involves a multiple set thorough assessment of the child's current social functioning. Knowing the root cause of social exclusion and the inability to effectively interact with others is vital as the treatment and measures taken depend on the exact problem. Exercises, drills, and group practice will vary depending on which social skills are in the biggest deficit. Furthermore, in some cases, the cause for social exclusion has to do with stigmatization and rejection from peers and communities around the child, which does not have anything directly to do with a deficit or lack of motivation to socialize on the part of the child.

Therapy and social skills programs also involve an analysis of whether there is a deficit in certain social skills or a lack of motivation for engagement in certain activities. Think of dynamic social environments like school, where a child has to interact with strangers. If there is a struggle in that area, this can be because of a deficit in social skills or because, for some reason, there isn't sufficient motivation to engage in that activity despite being capable of doing so. The final component that many professional courses consider is the role of the environment which shapes the performance and social skills of a person with ASD. On one hand, programs like peer training for teachers and autism awareness classes can be given to make the environment more accommodating for people on the spectrum while simultaneously training children to adapt and work in different social environments.

The holistic and meticulous approach of professionals is something that any parent, caretaker, and even an adolescent with ASD can keep in mind. Improvement is a gradual but not always linear process, meaning that there will be hardships and obstacles in the way. Knowing the strengths, weaknesses, and needs of a person means that specific goals, exercises, and drills can be crafted that address all of those while providing the ability for supervision, guidance, and support when challenges are encountered.

As children with ASD enter adolescence and begin to prepare themselves for adulthood, it's important to begin teaching them how to do this assessment by themselves. That's not to say that professional support should stop after a certain age, rather, it's to acknowledge their need for a greater degree of independence and help them in the process.

For example, a person on the spectrum can reflect on what are their strengths, weaknesses, and the corresponding goals they'd like to set for themselves. They reflect on their own by writing in their journal or on a document and conclude that they are very loyal to people and very interested in getting to know more about those they interact with, two great strengths they can use to deepen existing friendships and establish further ones. Nevertheless, they realize that they struggle to have a conversation with strangers that flows smoothly, and they don't feel very comfortable in social events and wish to change that, those are their new short-term goals.

A few weeks or months later, they've practiced talking to strangers and can now hold a conversation on their own but relaxing and feeling comfortable in social events hasn't changed much. Once a considerable amount of time has passed, they can assess the situation again, if social events feel very uncomfortable, they can limit them and promise to try again in the future. If they want to try a different approach, they can focus on social events with fewer people or bring friends along to make it more comfortable. Each goal and experience is a process of trial and error that ultimately relies on knowing what you want and reflecting from time to time on how that should influence your behavior and actions.

The Fundamental Rules of Social Interaction

Interacting meaningfully with others is a whole art containing hundreds if not thousands of facial cues, body language signals, and voice changes that one ought to keep in mind. What a glance to the side, crossed arms, or scratching one's nose means can vary across people, ages, and cultures, making the effort of reading people a nightmare for many people. Even if one becomes proficient in reading body language signals, there are hundreds of them, and you can't feasibly decipher everything in the span of 2 seconds you have before having to respond.

While many books and resources have been produced in recent years by experts on body language, and many suggest going through them and learning "how to read people," the unfortunate truth is that it's not feasible for the vast majority of people. When the way people express themselves is so complex, ambiguous, and hard to read, the solution is to simplify. You don't have to remember what every single body language signal, facial cue, or voice fluctuation means as long as you can broadly associate them with what kind of emotion they express. Some will definitely express negative emotions, discontent, frustration, discomfort, and many others. Others will certainly express positive emotions, happiness, excitement, and comfort, among many others.

Positive emotions are a signal that the person feels comfortable and eager to communicate and interact with somebody else, if that's the case, then no actions have to be taken, and both of them can relax and enjoy the interaction. Negative emotions like discomfort, discontent, frustration, and anger are a signal that there's something wrong that ought to be corrected. The question now is, which body language signals, facial cues, and voice changes show positive emotions and which ones show negative emotions?

Positive emotions can broadly be associated with body language signals and facial cues where a person opens up. A person scooting closer to you, leaning forward, or turning their body towards you along with their eyes fixated on you is a universally positive sign. If somebody feels close to other people and comfortable in their presence, then it makes sense to wish to be close to them as well. This also means that physical contact, like touching your knee or shoulder, is likely for a person who feels comfortable around you. Another positive sign is if a person seems curious, interested, and focused by keeping their head still and eyes on you, leaning towards you, and nodding along to what you are saying. Smiles and grins are one more way to see if a person enjoys talking and interacting with you, whether their lips are slightly tilted forward, or they are outright grinning and laughing, it's a sign that they feel content and comfortable with you.

Spotting negative emotions may be easier as there are many ways in which anxiety, frustration, discontent, and anger can manifest. When people are nervous, they usually touch the back of their neck or some area around their neck and rub their face, specifically their forehead, nose, and eyes. Nervousness can also make a person pace around, sway in their seat and tinker with their necklaces, rings, hair, or anything else around. Exasperation can be expressed in a similar way, but when people are frustrated, they also tend to purse their lips, exhale more sharply than usual and hold their breath for longer.

The biggest giveaway for negative emotions seems to be a closed body language, or when somebody's generally turned away from you, their feet are pointing somewhere else, they refuse to look at you at all or for more than a glance, and they turn themselves away from you with crossed arms. Usually, negative emotions are also accompanied by changes in verbal expression, a person's voice may grow more quiet and stiff, their replies shorter, and they may sound more passive or even dismissive when regarding you if they happen to feel frustrated or uncomfortable.

Even if all those body language signals can be summarized as either showing positive or negative emotions, it's still hard for a person to keep all of them in mind, especially during dynamic exchanges and fast-paced interactions. The best way to practice body language observation is to pick a single way in which people express themselves, for example rubbing their neck and to watch out for it in your own social interactions or intentionally try to spot it while watching movies and TV. With time and effort, being aware of other people's body language will become easier, and a person with ASD can learn to spot patterns and more quickly draw conclusions.

Learning to read facial and body language cues is just the first step, the next one is to adapt based on the response you receive from others. If, during an interaction, only positive emotions can be spotted, then everything is going well, and you can continue behaving in the way you had intended.

If something seems awry and a person displays negative emotions, then measures ought to be taken. Before getting too hasty and putting the blame on yourself, it's important to keep in mind the context in which an interaction is happening.

Context can mean both the environment in which it's happening and the specific time period. It may be that a friend is acting cold and discontent because of the loud environment around you or because a person with whom they are not in good relations has entered the room. Furthermore, aside from environmental cues which may trigger a negative reaction, the time in which you are interacting may affect how they are feeling. You may be doing your best to have a meaningful interaction, but if a person has just failed their exams or has family issues at home, then you are not to blame. If such a situation of discomfort arises, then consider if the topic you are talking about or the way you are handling the conversation may be a problem, trying to stir it in a different direction is preferable and if that doesn't work, then consider asking them what's wrong to learn what's bothering them outside the conversation.

Real interactions and conversations are very dynamic, the atmosphere can change very quickly, and spontaneous re-marks, expressions, and gestures are the norm as opposed to having the opportunity to be careful with every single reaction, remark, and move you are going to make. Even if that's the case, it can be immensely useful to know what your partner is feeling and over time to gradually learn how to read body cues and respond based on them. It's not a skill that a person can learn at once, it will take months and maybe even years of social interaction, but it's ultimately a worthy investment.

As a final note, it's important to keep in mind that the end goal of reading the body language and often cues that people provide is to have more authentic and meaningful relationships. To have such fulfilling relationships is to be open and vulnerable towards another person and to appreciate and love them for who they are. Using specific responses and expressions when certain facial cues or body language signs are given to steer people toward a certain response should not be done with the intention of manipulating others. It's not only immoral, and people who get into social skills training should be reminded of that often, but it's also ineffective as manipulation and lies are an unsustainable way to maintain closeness with another person, and eventually, they'd get discovered.

Encouraging Motivation and Curiosity

A person can rationally know that practicing an activity is good for them thus, they should dedicate time and effort to improve, but that doesn't mean they are emotionally invested in becoming better. In this particular instance, you may give a person with ASD many potential benefits of improving their social skills, but unless this connects to what they want and desire, then there's no guarantee that any approach, personal or professional, will be successful.

One effective way to bolster motivation is to rely on visualization. Making a person vividly and continuously imagine what the effort they are putting in will result in can be a powerful way to make them overcome doubt and anxiety over the short term and dedicate to long-term improvement. Instead of just sending them into group therapy or acting classes in high school, ask them how they'd like their social life to look like and connect their dreams and desires with those activities.

Another long-lasting way to spark change is by relying on curiosity. People with ASD tend to be extremely bright and full of interest in various hobbies, passions, and interests. If social skills are an issue, then you can turn the otherwise tedious lessons about contextual cues and body language into interesting quests and lessons. The next time you watch a movie, you can encourage them to ask questions about what social actions or moments from interactions they don't understand and then proceed to explain it to them, before you know it, they won't stop asking questions.

Curiosity and observation of the behavior of others can easily develop into a habit of being watchful for the way others behave in all sorts of situations. Making an intentional effort from time to time to discover how other people are behaving and trying to think through why they may be behaving and acting this way can be very useful and have compounding effects once it becomes a habit.

Motivating them to improve their social skills is not only about the lesson but the way it's presented. For many adolescents with ASD, using stories that have within themselves examples of social skills, rules and strategies can be an excellent way to keep them engaged. For the highest chance of success, the parent or caregiver can pick from the books and comics they are reading and the shows and movies they enjoy watching and look for lessons that can be presented. This is not only a very engaging way to present social lessons, but it can also bring everybody closer together.

One final way to encourage improvement in social skills is through groups dedicated to those activities. One guaranteed benefit is the exposure to experts and professionals who specialize in assessing the weaknesses, strengths, and needs of every person and then accommodating based on that. A secondary benefit related to motivation is the way building a sense of community and belonging to a group can encourage a person with ASD to keep coming back and to learn while having fun and enjoying themselves.

Leveraging a Person's Unique Personality

So much talk about flaws, hardships, and challenges that one must overcome can easily make everybody believe that being on the spectrum is a curse that you have to somehow mitigate and fix. There's nothing broken that ought to be fixed about having ASD, and in spite of the challenges that those with the condition encounter, there's much more to a person than just the obstacles they may face. Each adolescent with ASD is a unique person with their own vibrant and charming personality who has their own strengths, passions, and interests that make them much more than just an individual who's on the spectrum.

Knowing that and constantly making sure that the person with ASD remembers that very well is vital as a way to boost their self-esteem and confidence. Having faith in yourself and knowing that you are valuable is necessary for a person to engage in interactions with others meaningfully. Constantly putting yourself down and thinking that everything about you is unworthy of interest and appreciation can discourage people from interacting with you or may, ironically, prevent them from being exposed to everything that there is to love about you.

Friendships and other relationships across life are often formed based on the interests of a person. It's the mutual interest and passion for a subject that two people have which makes talking relatable, fun, and enjoyable. Even if interests don't align, being able to confidently express your thoughts and opinions and share what you are interested in speaks of a person with a strong and authentic personality that is seen as attractive and respectable by others.

The parents and caregivers of adolescents with ASD should make sure to promote those strengths, passions, and interests and to ensure that they aren't perceived as "weird over-fixating," "bizarre obsessions," or anything that brings shame or guilt. Interests not only help a person find and forge meaningful relationships with others, but they are also a great source of personal fulfillment and discovery about themselves and the world.

A final note ought to be made on how a person with ASD can leverage even the hardships they experience in a positive way. Struggling to communicate an idea or forgetting to do something can be followed through with a self-aware joke. Taking over a conversation and hyper-focusing on a particular topic you are passionate about can be followed with a sincere apology in which you also mention that you got carried away because you love this subject so much. Laughing in the face of hardships and embracing your unique challenges can not only build a person's confidence but it's also hugely empowering.

Dealing With Negative Emotions And Maintaining Motivation

Interactions and communication with others are not always a positive experience, often, the aftermath can leave a person dissatisfied, frustrated, and overwhelmed with everything that ought to be done just to maintain good relations with another person. When hardships and challenges are often present, it can wear down a person emotionally and remove their motivation to try and improve.

One major source of negativity happens to be anxiety and fear, which can hinder interactions or make a person doubt how they are perceived and liked afterward. Sometimes fear and anxiety can be so intense that they prevent a person from engaging in interactions altogether as they become very risk-averse and prefer not to take the chance to be embarrassed and ashamed of themselves.

Dealing with severe anxiety may require therapy and assistance from qualified professionals, but there are also personal measures that can be taken to lessen how huge of a hold it has over a person's actions. Fighting anxiety begins with the recognition that not all or even many of the fears we have are legitimate. Human brains have developed stress and fear as mechanisms that optimize a person's body for survival, if somebody is anxious, they are constantly alert to danger, and they wish to run away to escape from potential danger. Just because the body can't tell the difference between a bear that wants to tear you apart and a social event full of strangers doesn't mean the mind can't make an effort to break from that illusion.

The sheer recognition that there is nothing to be afraid of can be a powerful way to reduce anxiety for many people. For others, specific techniques may be more efficient, such as trying to slow down your breathing and focus on the interactions in the present instead of over-thinking what other people may be thinking while you are talking with them. There are also ways to reduce anxiety before and after interacting with others, prior to a social event or a meeting with friends, you can think of your anxiety as excitement for the upcoming meeting, the body reaction is the same, but now it's perceived as an actual positive. After an interaction, you can try and focus on the positive instead of dwelling on what may have gone wrong.

Feeling down and demotivated can often happen as progress in social interactions can be slow or stagnant for certain periods. Negativity can become especially haunting as a consequence of failure or rejection from a person or a community. Regaining your confidence starts by recognizing that progress in recent days or weeks may not have been huge, but it's nevertheless an improvement that wouldn't exist otherwise. Furthermore, oftentimes people tend to compare themselves with what they want to be or with others without making an effort to recognize who they were at the beginning of their journey and how far they've come. Finally, when it comes to failures and disappointments, it's important to take a breath and acknowledge that it happened but keep in mind that it's not the end of the world, and there will be many other opportunities to try again, be better and reach your goals.

Sometimes no matter the strategies and mindset adjustments a person makes, feeling anxious, overwhelmed, and exhausted can't be avoided. While people speak of fatigue, the first thought that comes to mind is often a person who's sweating and ready to collapse due to physical labor. Many dismiss or don't recognize altogether how exhausting social interactions can be, especially when you are out of your zone of comfort and trying to improve by paying attention to so much at once.

In spite of the mantra for consistency and continuous practice and experiment both for communication and social skills in general, it's important for a person with ASD to be taught and encouraged to express when they are feeling exhausted and to take breaks. Simply playing your favorite video games, listening to an album that brings you comfort, or diving deep into a hobby or passion of yours can all be ways to recharge your batteries when nothing else quite works.

One final note must be made on the need to be mindful and critical of the people with whom you surround yourself. Facing hardships and challenges with social skills can make people on the spectrum prone to try and befriend everybody, having doubts about your self-worth and value as an individual may make you more willing to accept all kinds of relationships even if the other person is not treating them as well as they should be.

Knowing your own worth and being confident that your strengths, passions, and interests combine into an amazing person is essential to remember on its own, but it should also serve as a way to defend yourself from people who may not have your best intentions in mind. People with ASD should be taught to value themselves and not be excessively selfless and loyal to those that don't reciprocate, and to be mindful of characteristics and types of behavior that can hint toward long-term problems in friendships and romantic relationships such as dishonesty and lack of commitment.

Chapter Four

Regulation Skills

R egulation is the ability of a person to channel their thoughts, emotions, and mental capacity to allow them to pursue their goals and improve their life. Self-regulation involves controlling your arousal levels to stimulate yourself by the environment and taking action, self-restricting and re-channeling your emotions in more beneficial ways, and using the mental processes required to concentrate, plan and solve problems in your head.

People on the spectrum tend to have differences in their brain structure, particularly in the prefrontal cortex responsible for executive function. Executive function is an umbrella term for all functions required for a person to effectively engage with a task and pursue their goals.

Impairments in executive function can involve any of the following abilities to varying degrees: finding the motivation to start with a task, having the short-term working memory to remember the details of a task, keeping your attention channeled on the task and not wandering off, being able to plan and visualize what ought to be done and the end result and self-monitoring and controlling oneself to prevent impulses and emotions from getting in the way.

Issues with executive function are not inherent and unique only to ASD, other conditions such as ADHD experience difficulties with executive function to varying degrees. This is why around 30 to 80% of children on the spectrum are also eligible for diagnosis with ADHD, and vice versa, 20 to 50% of children with ADHD are eligible to be diagnosed with ASD. ADHD is often stereotyped as a condition involving impulsive children who can't stay still, but the inability to retain attention, lack of motivation for tasks, and emotional dysregulation are all hardships that a person with ADHD experiences and somebody with ASD may experience in a similar way. Here are some of the struggles related to regulation:

- Inability to regulate sensations results in sensory overload, where a person feels overwhelmed by certain sounds, textures, smells, tastes, and sensations altogether.

- Emotional dysregulation can present itself in tantrums, breakdowns, and exaggerated emotional reactions that are not appropriate to the context of the situation.

- A lack of self-control and inhibition can lead to impulsive and poorly thoughts out decisions.

- A lack of motivation and the ability to act can lead to disorganization and procrastination.

Dealing With Emotional Dysregulation

Emotional dysregulation can feel like driving a car, but suddenly your hands go numb, and you can't operate the wheel anymore. You are either completely incapable or barely able to stir the wheel and direct where your thoughts and emotions will be going for a certain amount of time. While in some cases, an emotional outburst happens as a consequence of stress, fatigue, and mental exhaustion building up other times, it can happen so suddenly that there's barely any time to react.

Emotional dysregulation does not have a single universal way in which it manifests, exaggerated emotional reactions can appear in many different ways. Throwing a tantrum or breaking down after being denied something they want, getting very gloomy after even a mild constructive suggestion during a conversation, laughing far longer than others at a joke, or crying uncontrollably at a sad scene during a movie, are all just some of many cases in which emotions can go out of control.

Parents and caregivers should be there to assist teens on the spectrum in dealing with emotional dysregulation by observing which environments or specific experiences are likely to lead to issues of emotional dysregulation. Make a list of every single experience you can think of, and then connect it to the reaction that the child on the spectrum has had. The scale could be from 1 to 5 or 1 to 10 based on the seriousness and severity of the reaction. What matters the most is that issues of emotional dysregulation are tracked, especially negative reactions to the same experience that repeat over time.

There are clear reasons why social rejection from peers, sudden changes in routine, and having to talk to strangers may lead to emotional turmoil. Such issues can be addressed by creating a more safe and accommodating environment, where people are more accepting and comforting to the needs of the person with ASD. Another solution is to rely on a slow and gradual introduction, rebukes, and constructive criticism over behavior can be made more gently if harsh critique produces an adverse reaction. In a similar way, introduction to strangers, different routines, and unfamiliar environments can be done in a controlled environment with the assistance of a therapist, counselor, and other qualified professionals.

One crucial aspect of managing emotional dysregulation is the ability to understand your own emotions. Not all emotional outbursts or burnouts happen suddenly; there's usually a build-up where a person can feel the emotional and mental fatigue stacking up and can see themselves growing more prone to frustration and impulsivity. Having a better understanding of how you are feeling can be essential for taking preventive measures to avoid emotional turmoils altogether or to better understand what led to them and better manage the aftermath of one. Learning to understand and question how you are feeling and why you are feeling this way is best done with the assistance of qualified professionals with lots of experience and science-based methods.

Counseling and therapy can also be accompanied by personal exercises such as journaling, where a person reflects on how they are feeling and explores their emotions. Non-intrusive and supportive questions from parents and caregivers encouraging the child to express how they feel can also be a valuable way to express their feelings better. When it comes to vulnerability, especially in front of people whom you care about, it's best to lead by example. As a parent and caregiver, you should clearly express how you feel in the aftermath of a situation or share other experiences where you've struggled and worked hard to come to terms with your emotions, it's not only a sign of vulnerability that encourages the child to reciprocate and share but it also makes them feel less alone because they are not the only person going through such distress.

Learning to understand and communicate your emotions well is the first step toward preventing emotional outbursts and turmoils when anxiety, fatigue, and other negative emotions begin to pile up. It's important to allow a child with ASD and not discourage them from changing their behavior if they begin to feel overwhelmed. Being an open and social person may be preferable in most cases, but reducing eye contact, turning away from others for a time, or preferring solitude for a brief time altogether is preferable for them to recharge their social and emotional battery. Furthermore, many people on the spectrum happen to be very empathetic, so solitude and time away from others may be necessary as the feelings and emotions of others tend to rub off on them very intensely.

Knowing how you are feeling and what leads to emotionally overwhelming situations can be effective in taking preventive measures in certain situations, but it's also useful as a way to deconstruct emotions afterward. Take, for example, rejection sensitivity, which is the tendency of people to react with excessive negativity if facing critique or mild negative responses from people around them. The feeling of rejection is quite exaggerated, being able to comprehend that it's out of touch with reality won't make it disappear altogether, but it can help better manage the aftermath of such situations by knowing it's not the end of the world.

Emotional dysregulation can also be addressed by making changes to the way in which you are leading your day. Having fun, enjoying yourself, and chasing passions and interests is one sure way to relax and release some of the pressure from the day. Getting so caught up in schoolwork or other responsibilities, especially if you happen to be a perfectionist, can make you avoid or forget to take breaks. As a parent or caregiver, it's important to look over the child and make sure that they are setting boundaries between the time that's been committed for work and other responsibilities and the time which should go towards resting.

Children can be forgetful or, due to a low sense of self-worth, may wish to compensate for perceived flaws by pursuing personal and academic success, this is why it's so important to intervene and prevent burnout. If they don't understand the need for breaks, it's best to explain to them why the more you work during the day, the less each additional hour of work adds value to your projects or responsibilities as you grow more mentally and physically tired. Furthermore, they may push themselves to the maximum some days, but if they become too exhausted and burn out, then they won't have the will and motivation to do work tomorrow in the next few days.

Taking a break can happen as part of a day, but you could also dedicate a whole day for relaxation as well. There will inevitably be some blue days where nothing seems to be going right, and the child doesn't appear able to remain productive or make progress in any skills or projects they have. If that's the case, you can relieve them from responsibilities and allow them to immerse themselves in a hobby or a passion of theirs. You can take time off to go outside, someplace they adore and would bring them lots of joy, or you can remain in your home and play games or watch movies together. As a parent and caregiver, it must be important to have your child be productive, manage their time well, and succeed in order to prove the prejudice of the world wrong, but it's even more important to realize that they have a value outside of achievement and above anything else they should feel comfortable and happy.

Blue days and periods where not everything is going great are inevitable, outside of the fun and enjoyable activities, it's important for the child to have a place where they can express and vent their emotions. Going to therapy with a qualified professional who has experience dealing with similar cases can be life-changing as they can combine compassion and care along with expertise on the subject. Sometimes a child may not feel comfortable sharing with professionals, so the parents and other caregivers should be there to provide emotional support. In other cases, the child does not wish to share with anybody else altogether, reminding them of the need to open up may be helpful, but it can also lead to further isolation. When nothing else works, remember that there are ways to express how you feel even in solitude, such as journaling. They are not only better than not doing anything to understand and come to terms with your emotions, but once a child opens up on paper or on a document, they will be more willing to share with others. Very often, it's not the lack of willingness to share but the struggle to express and come to terms with their emotions that prevents communication on such issues.

All the measures provided so far, to some degree, rely on the person learning to better express their emotions and acknowledge that they exist. Nevertheless, many people on the spectrum struggle with a chronically low sense of self-worth and a lack of confidence. The exact reasons vary from person to person, but the unique challenges they experience and stigmatization, judgment, or rejection from peers, communities, and society as a whole can make them doubt their value as a person. In many cases, persons on the spectrum feel broken, as if there is something missing that needs to be added, or they should find a way to "fix" themselves and become neurotypical like everybody else. Such a belief is not only unachievable as ASD is an irreversible change to the structures of the brain, but it's toxic because it serves to constantly undermine a person's dignity.

As parents and caregivers, it's important to promote beliefs and mindset adjustments that fight such harmful narratives and allow the child to live in a way without feeling as though there's a fundamental flaw or a missing piece that ought to be fixed in them.

First and foremost, children should gradually be taught to radically accept their circumstances. Radically accepting yourself, with all the challenges and hardships you've endured along with all quirks, strengths, passions, and interests, is the most effective way to prevent denial and the need to "fix" yourself. It's a non-judgemental look at who you are, not saying that your life is negative or positive, rather, it's about embracing your circumstances and working from there with no shame or guilt that you haven't fixed yourself.

Second, once adolescents learn to accept their condition without ascribing negative values towards themselves, it's time to show them everything there is to love, appreciate and be interested in about their personality and how who they are may be influenced by their condition but does not define them. Practicing compassion and self-love begins with parents and caregivers encouraging such a mindset and continues with them teaching the child how to hold onto such beliefs by themselves.

Finally, adolescents with ASD should be taught a growth mindset even for issues related to emotional dysregulation. Feeling overwhelmed and out of control is a soul-crushing experience, it's not only better to strive to improve the situation bit by bit over the long term, but it's also vital for people to have a sense of hope and autonomy over their lives when they feel as though they have no control over their thoughts and emotions.

Finding Motivation and Overcoming Procrastination

Everyone suffers from a lack of motivation and procrastination to some degree, but impairments in executive function can make it comparatively harder for people on the spectrum to manage unpleasant work, remain focused on the task, and not procrastinate until the last moment on assignments and responsibilities.

Procrastination is an issue that can have many potential reasons for occurring. The most simple one is that the task that ought to be done just doesn't make you feel good. A school assignment that's tedious, on a boring subject, and that's imposed on you as an obligation that diminishes any trace of intrinsic motivation is sure to lead to procrastination. You probably can realize that the assignment must be completed, but how you feel hasn't quite caught up yet, if you have a week before the deadline, you rationally know it's time to work, but the unpleasant feeling of dealing with the task is much higher than any gratification or relief you will feel if you start. It's only during the last hours before a deadline that the consequences become much more clear and stark that you start working and manage to complete the assignment.

Another reason for procrastination is delaying a task due to perfectionism. Ironically, being a perfectionist means you become fearful of failure and want to do everything perfectly. Many people who are perfectionists end up excessively planning and theoretically trying to figure out a task instead of starting at all, or they just avoid it altogether in spite of wanting to start because tying your sense of self-worth to the success in a task means it becomes much more intimidating. Once the stakes are higher, anxiety, frustration, and doubt begin to overtake your judgment, and starting becomes much harder.

One misconception about work is that you ought to start with what's hardest and that the work process itself is one where you ought to be productive through and through until you reach the desired result. In reality, starting smaller and more manageable tasks can be a great way to warm up and get in the zone for work. Furthermore, no matter the work that you are doing, school assignments, extracurriculars, or other responsibilities, work is a process of discovery where you get better and learn more about the task at hand and how to complete it while working. Being afraid of failure or making mistakes actively prevents you from doing a task in the most effective way and can, ironically, stop you from trying to do the task altogether.

If there is one huge project that is due in two weeks, the easiest way to start working on it is to break it down into smaller tasks. By itself, the project feels challenging, intimidating, and even overwhelming. The bigger the project, the more threatened you are likely to feel by what's required of you and the more unclear it may be how you are supposed to proceed. Breaking down the project means you can start with smaller tasks to warm up and take it step by step while also having a very clear vision of what the current step is and what will be required next. Taking it step by step is also useful when you are not up for long working sessions, instead of trying to tackle the whole project, you can take one small milestone and complete it so that some progress has been made instead of none at all.

Finally, smaller tasks can be hugely motivating as they give a clear sense of accomplishment, feeling as though you've achieved something is one effective way to boost your motivation and continue towards the next task. People usually think of motivation as your ability and desire to take action, but there is an inverse connection as well. If you are intentional in your efforts and take action, soon enough, you will get motivated and start a positive loop that keeps you going. Although breaking down a task into smaller ones and planning prior to that how you will handle an assignment for the sake of clarity is immensely useful, you should be careful not to excessively plan and think it through to the point of procrastinating on starting the task itself.

Regulating your behavior to start and remain on a task can be very challenging if the environment is not suitable for work. Your senses can't just be turned off, so being in a room full of noise may not remove your ability to concentrate altogether, but it's a constant mental strain to retain your attention. Usually, the best environments are those where distractions are minimized, with no background noises or anything happening in your surroundings. Relying on sound-isolating headphones and removing any noise from the room is one sure way to minimize distractions.

Very often, people work on their laptops and computers, so social media and access to the internet, both on the device and on the nearby phone, can be a massive source of distraction. If a task happens to be tedious or challenging, it's hard to explain to your stimulation craving brain why you can't just scroll through videos on Youtube for the next few hours instead of studying. This is why applications that block social media or outright removing your phone from the room can reduce temptations very effectively. You can also rely on promises for rewards, if the temptation to scroll social media will always be a part of the environment, then you can promise yourself that you have 10 minutes for a Youtube video once this particular part of the assignment is completed.

Environments not only influence your ability to be motivated and productive because of the way they interact with your senses but also because we tend to associate places with certain activities. If somebody were to ask you what's the function of a gym, you'd instantly say to train. Likewise, if somebody asked you what you'd go to the library for, most would reply to read and study. In a similar way, you can teach a person with ASD to separate places or parts of a room so that each one can be exclusively associated with a singular activity. Studying on your bed is not preferable if you also tend to relax and sleep on it, instead, you should make it a habit to study on the desk so that it's associated with work. If the whole room is distracting, then studying in the park, library, or somewhere else quiet can also be an effective way to get work done.

One final way to control your motivation and ability to be productive has to do with your mindset. One essential belief to rid yourself of is perfectionism. Being a perfectionist creates a false expectation that the first draft of an assignment should be flawless or that you'd be able to finish the work in a single session with barely any distractions. The high standard created by perfectionism's not only unattainable in the vast majority of cases, but it's also very much overwhelming and paralyzing. Even if one wishes to be as productive as possible, perfectionism doesn't provide this because it makes you averse to risks, experimentation, and making mistakes is the ultimate way for you to become more productive and more proficient in what you are doing. Finally, no matter the result, a child who always strives for perfection will have a low sense of self-worth and confidence because no matter how much they do, it's never enough.

A second mindset change to consider is the need to practice self-compassion and forgiveness. People tend to be their own harshest critics, especially when they think there's something wrong, flawed, or broken about them that ought to be fixed by work, accomplishments, and tireless effort. Children with ASD should be encouraged to do their best, but they should be content with what they have done for the day and be proud of themselves and what has been achieved, even if the result isn't perfect. Self-compassion is also about forgiving yourself, some days, you just don't have the physical, mental or emotional ability to do certain tasks or to complete as much as you may have wanted. On such occasions, it's not your fault, and you shouldn't be treating yourself harshly, forgiving yourself and promising to get back to what had to be done eventually is a much more helpful and healthy way to cope with hardships.

So far, we've discussed strategies to make yourself more motivated, and productive and develop healthy mindsets about work. Sometimes when no individual strategy or intrinsic desire works, it's effective to also rely on automatic systems of regulation. The first type of system is one that people set for themselves. To do-lists, setting a deadline for a task or asking the teacher to create a firm deadline, and relying on alarms and reminders can all be effective ways to keep the task in mind and create a sense of urgency. Systems of regulation and accountability can also be related to other people. Adolescents can be kept accountable for their tasks by parents and caregivers who make sure they are on track with their studies, responsibilities, and other goals while also providing guidance and emotional support when needed. Many find it immensely helpful and effective to find accountability partners where a friend or a relative around your age works alongside you daily, or you both check up on each other every day or a few times a week to see how you are both progressing in your goals.

Managing Impulsivity

Impulsive decisions are one where an action is taken based on an impulse, instinct, or a hunch without the person being able to carefully consider whether or not the action is beneficial for them. Many people with ASD are extremely self-aware, careful, and cautious when making decisions, but that doesn't mean they are not prone to moments where impulsive decisions take over. Impulsivity can manifest in many ways, such as the inability to wait in lines, abruptly interrupting conversations, or buying items without consideration for how their pocket money ought to be spent.

Dealing with impulsivity should start from the ground up by explaining the problem with impulsive actions, as that's not a given for every child with ASD to understand. Sometimes it's hard to realize what effect a sudden interruption when somebody's talking has on the person, or they can't see the reason as to why a certain object shouldn't be bought the moment they want it. Explain the long-term consequences of their actions and why even if they want to do something in the present, it may not be the best way to satisfy their desires or reach their goals down the line.

Impulsivity in adolescents can lead to many addictive behaviors like obsessions with junk food or video games. More conservative approaches relied on severely restricting or outright banning such experiences because they were seen as harmful. If a child is likely to indulge in them excessively out of an impulse or inability to control their impulses, then removing them altogether should do the trick. Unfortunately, such measures don't take into account that the child can't always be supervised and that, over the long term, they will grow into independent adults who haven't been taught how to manage such potentially addictive behavior. When it comes to following your impulse towards such enjoyable activities, the rule should be moderation. Having their favorite treat should not happen every day, but it can happen after performing well at school or improving in a certain area of life. In much the same way, video games can become a fulfilling reward and a way to relax after doing all your homework and work for the day.

Impulsivity is very hard to stop if you can't self-monitor or restrain yourself, which is why accountability mechanisms can be very effective both in adolescence and adulthood. People on the spectrum can make it a habit to talk with a trusted companion, a parent, caregiver, or a friend before making a decision. One similar strategy is to allow themselves a week before taking a decision or making a purchase and informing somebody close to them to make sure they don't pre-emptively make a choice. Taking such measures isn't about stopping yourself from making decisions, but it serves as a way to get the perspective of somebody else and to have enough time to ponder on that action and fully figure out whether or not this is something you want to do.

The Importance of Healthy Lifestyle Choices

Having ASD is not a condition that can be reversed no matter the lifestyle choices and healthy habits that you develop. Nevertheless, making sure to exercise often, have a healthy diet, and sleep well can vastly improve your physical and mental condition.

Exercise can single-handedly change the life of a person, not only physically but also mentally. Most exercise forms release endorphins which can reduce stress, enhance alertness and improve your mood. Exercising also encourages your body to produce and release neurotransmitters like dopamine which increase motivation and concentration and improve brain function. Aside from the benefits to your cognition, exercise is a great way to express yourself and release pent-up emotions. Frustration, anger, or any negative emotions don't have to be stigmatized and ignored, rather, there are healthy ways through which physical activity can help a person blow off some steam.

In a similar way, having a healthy diet is essential to your well-being. What you eat and what you don't can greatly influence your hormones and metabolism and, in turn, change your mental capacity and how you feel throughout the day. Which diet works best for a person with ASD depends on which foods they can tolerate because of sensory overload and distaste for certain smells, textures, and tastes. When deciding which food regime to try, it's best to consult a medical professional to inform yourself of the different options. There is no singular best diet, what works best can be discovered through trial and effort.

The general rule is that healthy diets are balanced, providing the ability to consume vegetables, fruits, meats, fish, and different types of seeds and nuts. Furthermore, food regimes shouldn't be excessively restricting and extreme in their approaches. Some may find results on a ketogenic diet where carbs are severely restricted, but that's far from advisable for adolescents who are still growing up. Furthermore, restrictive diets are often challenging because they are not sustainable, constantly experiencing hunger pangs and impulses for certain treats eventually wears down a person, and the relapse and over-eating that follows can wipe out any prior benefits.

Arguably the most important component of a healthy life is sleeping well. Poor sleep can have devastating consequences on the ability to function properly. Feeling more aggravated and more prone to impulsive decisions, experiencing more mood swings and a reduced capacity to regulate emotions and thoughts, and reduced alertness and concentration are just some of the many consequences that a poor sleeping schedule leads to. As you can probably guess, the negative consequences relate to challenges people with ASD are already experiencing to some degree, so not getting enough sleep will only exacerbate those symptoms even more.

Making sure a person is sleeping well begins with crafting a routine. Each person has a circadian rhythm that keeps their body in balance by automating body functions and tuning them into a routine. Going to sleep and waking up roughly at the same time will get the body used to that schedule, and it will become much easier to fall asleep and wake up at the reoccurring times. This way, the quantity, and quality of sleep increase overall.

Sometimes even with a routine, falling asleep can be troublesome. If somebody struggles to fall asleep, this may be because of stimulation through social media, video games or homework, and assignments that are being done at the last moment. If you are anxious and have tons of thoughts and emotions swirling in your mind then falling asleep can be nearly impossible. This is why it's best to have a clear end to work or any very stimulating types of behavior so that a person can relax for at least one or two hours before going to sleep.

One final obstacle to keep in mind is blue light. A person's circadian rhythm signals that it's time to sleep once the sun is gone from the sky but having lights everywhere shining on your face means your circadian rhythm doesn't give the signal because your body can't tell the difference. Turning off the lights as much as possible and reducing phone and computer usage can all be effective ways to tune in your body for sleep.

When it comes to healthy lifestyle choices, mindfulness is one more practice that can be considered in professional or personal settings as a way to better control impulses and regulate thoughts and emotions. In short, mindfulness is a non-judgmental observation of one's internal experiences, thoughts, and emotions. Mindfulness drills or meditation practices usually involve having an anchor, for example, your breathing, that a person focuses upon. The point isn't to never get distracted and have an unwavering concentration, rather, it's to bring your attention back to the anchor once it happens to drift off.

While a person focuses on their breathing, emotions will continue to flood their mind, and thoughts will keep swirling. Trying to ignore them, or even worse, to violently push them back, only makes them come back stronger. The point of mindfulness and meditation, in general, is to acknowledge what you feel instead of hopelessly trying to repress it. Learning to understand your thoughts and emotions non-judgementally can also mean that you won't get caught up in them, believing that the world or others perceive you in a certain way just because of irrational feelings. Finally, mindfulness can be immensely helpful for impulse control as it requires a person to intentionally train their concentration and refrain from actions that happen spontaneously.

Mindfulness shouldn't be seen as a complicated and unsustainable practice because the basics can be learned by anybody. Most mindfulness practices involve being in a quiet environment and sitting still with a straight back while choosing one type of sensation to focus upon as an anchor. Many prefer their breath or heartbeat as they are constantly reoccurring sensations that are easy to track and focus upon. How much a single session lasts depends on the person, most start with just five minutes a day and gradually increase the count over time.

Just as with other habits, the point is to maintain consistency over the long term. You shouldn't be shaming yourself and getting discouraged if some days there is no time or mental energy to meditate, especially if you are irritated and fatigued from the day before. Mindfulness and meditation can be forged as habits if done with other people as a group practice and also when added up to an already existing routine. People with ASD crave consistency and routines, so adding a short meditation session can be very effective in sticking with the habit if they find it beneficial.

Finally, it's important to keep in mind that there's no single right way to meditate. A mindfulness session doesn't mean you can't get distracted and sidetracked by rubbing your eyes or readjusting your body. For some standing still altogether doesn't work, so other forms of the practice like mindfulness walking can also be beneficial and much more sustainable.

Successful self-regulation requires personal and professional guidance to assist a person in learning which types of behavior they struggle to control. Once the person with ASD and their parents and caregivers have properly assessed the situation then a wide variety of strategies and systems can be implemented to improve self-regulation or to craft mechanisms that altogether bypass weak points.

Chapter Five

Memory skills

Having a strong memory is important for every aspect of a person's life. Remembering details of conversations that happened recently, keeping in mind all recent information related to a project in school or at work, and showing up for upcoming meetings are all just some of many examples in which a sharp memory is important for optimal functioning.

People on the spectrum don't just experience issues with memory as a whole, rather, specific types of memory may be impaired while they simultaneously excel at others far beyond the level of neurotypical people. Recognizing the nuances of memory is important to properly give personal and professional guidance and support towards the issue.

Differences Between Working Memory And Long-Term Memory

Issues with memory for people on the spectrum can often seem paradoxical. On one hand, a person with ASD may have fantastic long-term memory, they remember niche details from events and conversations that have happened weeks or even months ago. They also often have an encyclopedic knowledge of their passions, hobbies, and many other topics of interest. On the other hand, people on the spectrum can be very forgetful, unable to retain the information they were given minutes ago, forget obligations and generally be very disorganized.

Both those traits are not mutually exclusive, but many people can't comprehend the difference and, in turn, treat people on the spectrum with confusion, frustration, and anger because they struggle with seemingly trivial and small tasks. It's not easy to explain how niche information such as a long password for an old social media account can be remembered while where the keys have been stashed is a mystery that can't be solved even if it happened an hour ago.

The nuance in functioning has to do with the difference between verbal and non-verbal working memory and long-term memory. While the first serves to guide a person throughout the day, having recently absorbed information on standby to be used, the other looks more like a comprehensive archive of past events and experiences. People with ASD usually have strong long-term memory but may experience various unique challenges with working memory due to impairments in executive function.

As a parent or a caregiver, it's vital to acknowledge the difference because this allows you to encourage the child to improve and take advantage of their excellent long-term memory while also working to improve their short-term working memory.

Improving Working Memory

The phrase "out of sight, out of mind" can be especially true for an adolescent with ASD who struggles with working memory. There is a wide variety of lifestyle choices, memory training methods, and systems of organization that can all be employed to improve short-term memory.

All healthy lifestyle choices discussed in the previous chapter, such as sleeping well, having a nutritious diet, exercising regularly, and practicing mindfulness, can all be immensely helpful in improving memory and, more broadly, the cognitive capacity of an individual. There are also specific habits and exercises like memory-based games such as crosswords and word-recall games that can be practiced in real life or through mobile apps to gradually improve short-term memory. Journaling and intentionally trying to recall your day can also be an effective way to practice your short-term memory.

All of those can enhance cognitive function and improve memory skills in particular, but they won't completely eliminate challenges, nor should they be considered capable of doing so. Even if there is a limitation to how much short-term memory can be improved, there are many strategies and systems of organization and management that can be employed to compensate for that.

The issue of impaired working memory hinders the ability of a person to keep available information in the short term that they'd need to use throughout the current or following days, so systems and strategies should be designed to bypass the forgetfulness and ensure the information remains stored somewhere where it can be accessed again. An effective system would also be one where the important information can easily be stored, navigated, and has mechanisms to remind the person that the information is there and ought to be checked again.

For example, if you were to begin to teach a person with ASD how to better keep track of upcoming events and bypass their forgetfulness, you can create a digital calendar. Once an event appears on the horizon, they can add it to the calendar, which makes it clear what's coming up and where it's placed, among other obligations. Preferably such a system would also have an alarm or some kind of reminder to warn of the upcoming event or give the person a heads up to check the calendar every single day. Sophistication here isn't needed, you can experiment and try different mobile apps or just have a Google Sheet serving as a calendar and a daily alarm on your phone to remind you to check the calendar for upcoming events. What can be written in there? Appointments to therapists and weekly check-ups with medical professionals are two of many reoccurring events that can be clearly scheduled every single week automatically, so it becomes very clear and almost a routine that those activities are coming up.

The first step towards such an effective system would be automating as much as possible and acting on the spot. If an event or an obligation pops up in your calendar, it's best to quickly write it down to prevent accidents where you get distracted and forget about it altogether. The reminders a person sets for themselves are as simple as an alarm going off every single day reminding you to check the calendar or scheduling an email to yourself with very specific instructions and thoughts on what must be done on this specific day.

What should be remembered isn't always an upcoming event or responsibility, sometimes a person has an idea that they wish to develop further for a project or an assignment they are having, or they just want to remember a book they were recommended or an album they wanted to listen to. No matter what should be remembered, developing the habit of taking notes of everything is immensely useful. Which tool happens to be used in the end doesn't really matter as long as it's convenient to use and can be carried everywhere with the person.

A traditional paper notebook can work wonders, others prefer a note-taking application or a voice recorder which gives them more freedom to express themselves. It's not even necessary to stick with one way of taking notes as long as, in the end, a person manages to write down anything relevant that may need to be used down the line. Sometimes it may even be preferable to experiment, for example, by taking pictures instead of trying to record a voice message or write down something. If you leave your bike or car somewhere or if you want to remember an item you saw at the mall to later find something similar for a gift, then taking a picture is the most vivid way to remember the details and not waste time trying to remember.

Keeping track of everything relevant through notes can be effective in storing information, but the point of having information is for it to be easily accessible. This is why once a note or reminder is written, whenever you have the time, it should be revised again to clarify what its intended purpose is and to store it in a specific folder or category so that the whole system is easier to navigate. If the notes are later to upcoming events that are relevant only in the short term, then navigation is not that important, and periodically the notes that have become obsolete can be deleted altogether.

Teaching an adolescent with ASD to rely on external assistance to remember tasks can be encouraged if others participate in the system as well. One engaging way is to rely on whiteboards, sticky notes, or erasable markers, which can allow you to leave reminders or random notes to yourself or others throughout the house. Learning to write down what's on your mind takes practice for a person to feel comfortable doing that and to get used to automatically writing a note in the short span in which the specific event or information remains on top of their mind.

One last problematic aspect of forgetfulness is the way people with ASD may experience a distorted perception of time as they forget not only about obligations but lose track of time. A simple solution to that is having multiple clocks ready to display what's the current time. Having a wristwatch is comparatively better than using your phone, as the latter is full of distractions and temptations that can get you to procrastinate. Relying on alarms and reminding can also be a useful way to bypass time blindness and forgetfulness. If, despite everything, you are still late for assignments and responsibilities, consider making adjustments to your schedule a firm time in which you'd leave your home instead of trying to decipher when you'd be there and consider going out 10-15 minutes earlier than required to compensate for any delays.

Adolescence can often be viewed as one gigantic experiment where, through trial and error, teens discover who they are and test their abilities to effectively navigate the world and forge a path of their own. The pursuit of independence is a very important one, but that doesn't mean that one should strive to be completely independent of anybody else, especially if they happen to be struggling with certain tasks.

There's nothing shameful or embarrassing for a person to rely on friends, relatives, and partners for important appointments and responsibilities. The authentic and meaningful relationships we craft with one another exist so that people can help one another, and sometimes having another person by your side to assist you in the challenges you are facing is an effective and valid option to pursue.

Chapter Six

Personal safety

M any parents and caregivers who have been raising and looking after their children with ASD for many years are anxious to give them more independence due to the world's dangers. There's a prevalent perception that the world is a harsh, overwhelming, and dangerous place that can negatively affect you if you are not careful.

Interacting with the rest of the world is inevitable, especially when unforeseen and unexpected situations arise, so adolescents should gradually learn the basics of personal safety and how to manage the world without exposing themselves to dangerous situations as much as possible.

The Basics of Personal Safety

Teaching adolescents basic skills and techniques for personal safety should have ideally begun when they were younger. The basics include a very general understanding of situations that are dangerous and ought to be avoided, along with the knowledge of how to navigate them if the need arises. For example, if the siren for evacuation rings in school, they should know what has to be done.

When a dangerous situation arises, there is a very high chance that the appropriate authorities will show up. It's vital for a person with ASD to react appropriately either by not getting in the way or by co-operating with the authorities when the situation calls for it. First and foremost, they should very clearly understand the purpose of those institutions and how they are on their side and are solely there to keep them safe and to remove potential dangers. Second, they should be able to identify themselves by using their ID, reciting their personal information, or if they happen to get anxious, they should have everything written down. Any appropriate identification items such as ID and driver's license should always be in the same spot on them so that identification is as easy as possible. Finally, teens on the spectrum should be encouraged to evaluate situations in which the authorities were called and separately taught the scenarios in which they should be called so that they can request assistance from the police or firefighters or call an ambulance if the situation calls for it.

What personally feels frightening to people with ASD aren't only very dangerous situations but also ones with lots of ambiguity where they remain uncertain what precisely is expected from them. This is why it's vital for them to know the meaning of signs on the street - stop signs, exit signs, symbols for danger nearby, toilet signs, etc.

Common gestures by people, for example, those signaling you to wait, stop, and ask you something, should also be taught as they may be the reaction to a potentially dangerous situation that others should be wary of. Finally, it's also important to teach them the customs, rules, and expectations that each place and community you are going to expect from them.

Ideally, children should be taught all of that described above through direct guidance, work with professionals, and more interactive approaches such as role-playing and repetition of similar scenarios. Just imagining that you have to deal with authorities and trying to get in the shoes of a person who's in immense danger can feel very overwhelming and stressful. There is no guarantee that practice will instantly lead to results, but that shouldn't leave parents and caregivers discouraged. Multiple attempts should be made using various methods and approaches, and if that doesn't work, then consider coming back to the exercise in a few weeks or months. If at one point in time, they are not receptive, that doesn't mean that they will never be able to learn, which is why multiple attempts across time are essential.

One final point ought to be made about the need for a person to know how to defend themselves. No person wins physically or mentally if they try to confront another through violence and assault them, which is why fights and aggression should be discouraged. If a person actively displays aggression towards you, then it's advised to step away or even run away if they are holding dangerous weapons and ask for assistance from those nearby. Those are not always options which is why self-defense classes or picking up sports that allow you to defend yourself, in general, can be of great benefit.

First, they allow you the opportunity to learn various techniques and movements which can protect you if a confrontation becomes inevitable, and they also allow you to protect an innocent person if necessary. Second, being able to defend yourself and appearing as though you can stand your ground can de-escalate fights as this discourages an opponent from trying to hurt you. Third, the benefits of being able to defend yourself range far beyond what you may do in a potential confrontation, knowing you can stand your ground is a massive boost to your confidence and can serve to reduce anxiety in day-to-day life. Finally, becoming better at defending yourself can become a passion, the drills, exercises, discipline, and routine required may be deeply gratifying aside from providing lots of physical and practical benefits.

Preventative Measures To Maintain Safety

One of the most important measures for preventing danger is knowing how to adequately protect your home from unwanted visitors with potentially harmful intentions. Locking your door and closing your windows every time you go out can sound like basic, even trivial expectations to keep in mind since doing them is taken as a given, but if you happen to be in a rush or happen to be forgetful, then doing both of those may slip your mind.

For some on the spectrum who face severe difficulty with organization and remembering what ought to be done, having a small to-do list that ought to be completed before going out can be of huge assistance. For example, taking your purse with all essentials in it, making sure that the stove or anything else that may lead to a hazard is turned off, closing the windows, and locking the door. Eventually, all of this will become second nature, but it can be beneficial to go through the list from time to time if you are in a rush or happen to be anxious that you may forget something.

If an emergency happens at home, then you should have people whom you can call instantly for help. Depending on how urgent the situation is, parents or a close friend can be dialed, but if urgent actions need to be taken, then a trusty neighbor who's available and in close proximity can be very helpful as well. One final note on home safety has to do with who you allow in your home, people with ASD who are learning to manage on their own should know how to use peepholes and be taught rules on which people to welcome into their home.

The transportation system is one where dangers may arise, which is why supervision and constant guidance may be required in the beginning. For many people, one of the steps towards adulthood is learning to drive. Although teens with ASD may experience some struggle with learning this essential skill, this may be because they may just need a bit more time to familiarize themselves with the many complex factors at play. It's important to keep in mind that very often, purely the feeling of being overwhelmed, anxiety, and self-doubt can be a huge factor in whether or not you successfully learn a skill, so positive reaffirmation and encouragement may be necessary to boost their confidence and performance.

Driving may seem like a more challenging option, but public transportation can present its own unique issues for people on the spectrum. The cramped spaces, lack of personal space, loud and intruding noises, and unpleasant smells can all feel very overwhelming for people with ASD who are prone to sensory overload. Learning to handle public transit should happen gradually. First, they should learn the bus and subway lines that they will be using, then how to buy themselves tickets, use transportation cards and navigate tunnels, escalators, automatic doors, and how to read signs, bus and subway schedules, and maps. When it comes to sensory overload, relying on devices that reduce your sensitivity, like sound-isolating headphones, can be a potential solution. If possible, some find it most convenient to adjust their schedule and travel at times when traffic is not at its peak, and public transport is also not packed.

In all of the scenarios described above, it's essential for people on the spectrum to have guidance and support from parents and caregivers if any issue arises or they need practical advice on how to navigate certain situations. Once teens enter adulthood, the need for independence only grows stronger, and they may choose to rely more and more on themselves and on close friends. This is why it's important to assist teens with ASD in finding trustworthy friends that will be by their side if they happen to need assistance. Having such anchor friends can be especially helpful in foreign and unpredictable situations with many complex factors where reading context and social cues take a lot of time. For example, going to a social event in a new community can be overwhelming and hard to navigate, but having somebody to give you tips and assist you on the way can alleviate much of the anxiety and protect you from potential dangers.

Having The Right Mindset For Personal Safety

Teaching an adolescent about the importance of personal safety relies on finding a fine balance between the need for wariness and critical examination of situations and people and not overwhelming them with an excessively pessimistic perception of the world.

As a parent or caregiver who's seen what bullying, stigmatization, and dismissal from society looks like, it's easy to see why you'd be wary about the intentions of others toward your child. While a teen with ASD practices social skills, they should ideally also learn how to read the intentions of others. Whether it bullies or people who are trying to scam you, being harsh and rude or sometimes excessively flattering in a dishonest way, trying to extract personal information out of you, and coercing you into making promises and commitments even if you don't know them well enough are red flags that ought to be kept in mind.

The danger of being exploited is present not only in real life but very much in the digital realm as well, where anonymity and the ability to create fake profiles allow many people a much higher chance to sound convincing in the false narratives and stories they create. Stories, examples, and illustrations of such situations and instances should be clearly described to a person with ASD so they can imagine what the red flags look like and generally be wary of such sudden advances. Wariness does not mean that you have to be dismissive and afraid of every single interaction, rather, it gives you a few signs to look for and makes you think more critically of the intentions of other people since, unfortunately, not everybody is kind and selfless. Whenever a person on the spectrum experiences doubts and uncertainty about the intention of somebody, they know it's best to turn to parents, caregivers, or trusted close friends to help them read the contextual and social clues.

While wariness and a critical examination of the intentions people have may be required and necessary in many situations, it shouldn't turn into an obsession. Many people with ASD, alongside the condition, struggle with anxiety and social isolation, developing a belief that the world is full of solely horrible people, everybody has hidden, and malicious intentions and they are out to get you in one way or another can severely hurt your mental health. Having such a skewed perception of the world not only can sabotage existing friendships and the potential to grow and develop new ones, but it can also create an ever-present feeling of paranoia whenever you are and whatever you happen to be doing since there isn't a guaranteed way to constantly keep yourself safe.

This is why when teaching wariness, it's important to take a measured approach which requires a more critical look at the beginning of relationships rather than at all times and to clarify that questioning the intentions of others is necessary to filter out those who mean you harm, it doesn't mean that everyone is a horrible person.

Personal safety is one of the most essential skills that a person with ASD can be taught as it requires automatic and quick thinking which needs prior exercise and understanding of what ought to be done. Both as a reaction to adverse events and in taking preventative steps, people on the spectrum should be encouraged to critically examine the motives and intentions of those around them and to rely on assistance from trusted people around them if the situation calls for it.

Chapter Seven

Recreational skills

Recreational skills are essential for a person to properly rest, feel happy by themselves and with others, and meaningfully connect with people. People on the spectrum are flourishing individuals full of hobbies, passions, and interests which they develop and wish to express with others, but they may struggle to connect with others and effectively engage in communities related to their interests.

A holistic approach to recreational skills combines both professional and personal guidance to help children on the spectrum discover what brings them fulfillment, develop those hobbies and interests, and successfully join and be accepted by communities related to their passions.

The Importance of Recreational Skills

For the vast majority of the population, life is about finding something that gives you purpose, fulfillment, and happiness.

They either directly pursue hobbies and passions and build communities in their available time, or they make compromises, such as working hard to secure a more stable future for themselves and their family so that, over the long term, they can enjoy life.

People with ASD may suffer from anxiety, perfectionism, and low confidence, which means they are prone to prioritize academic and professional achievement at the expense of recreational skills. If they struggle to socialize with others and face rejection or dismissal from communities, they may turn even more sharply towards trying to find fulfillment in work instead of working on their recreational skills. In a society obsessed with productivity, constantly working and doing as much as possible, it's important to separate your worth as an individual from the amount of work you are doing and to realize that success in any area in life or hard work is some of the steps towards fulfillment but won't make you happy on their own.

Recreational skills are not only valuable as a source of happiness, but they are an activity in which a person can creatively express themselves. Creative trial and error, along with experimentation, are one of the best ways to learn more about yourself and your preferences. Looking at it this way, recreational skills are a tool for self-discovery where you learn more about yourself, what you value, what you enjoy, and what you want.

A final and often neglected benefit of recreational skills and activities is the need for you to fully rest and enjoy yourself, even those who are very competitive and goal-orientated can benefit from developing recreational skills and pursuing hobbies. In much the same way a person's physical body has a limit, so does their mind. Focusing solely on academic, professional, or other types of success makes a person may dampen a person's mood, make them more sensitive and impulsive and even lead to burnout. Hobbies, passions, and personal interests are all amazing ways to relax, have fun and enjoy yourself or in the company of others which can recharge your social and mental battery and ultimately makes you more productive.

Teaching a teen with ASD the importance of a healthy work-life balance and explaining to them the importance of recreational skills is vital to prevent toxic behavior that may hurt their physical and mental health down the line.

How To Develop Recreational Skills

It's important not to presume that all people have developed and well-defined interests and passions. Although children with ASD tend to have many hyper-fixations on certain subjects and topics or love certain hobbies, that doesn't necessarily mean this behavior label is applicable to everyone or that even those with well-defined interests can't benefit from guidance and support.

As parents and caregivers, you should be on the lookout for what makes the eyes of your child spark with excitement and joy since interest and passion correlate with opportunities to develop a part of what they love into a hobby or even a career. For example, if a child is fascinated with animated movies, they may have an interest in becoming a scriptwriter, animator, or artist. Even if that's not a career suitable for them, if they are curious enough, you can encourage them to try drawing and animating to see if they find enjoyment in it. Exploring that initial curiosity does not guarantee success, but only through this process of trial and error both of you can learn more about what the person with ASD truly enjoys.

All throughout the process, it's vital to remind them that there's no such thing as a "crazy obsession" or a "niche" and "boring" interest, even if others try to tell them otherwise, as long as they are fascinated by the subject and wish to learn more about that or to try it themselves then it's a valid passion to have.

Not all hobbies and interests can be pursued individually, playing games or sports with others requires the ability to effectively approach others, adapt to the rules of the game, and handle hardships, mistakes, and losses when playing with others. Approaching others and joining communities should be done in a polite, friendly, and non-intrusive way where the child shows interest in joining without making others feel forced or coerced into accepting them. People with ASD are usually quick learners, and they easily follow the rules, so the adaption process shouldn't take very long as long as the expectations, both of the game itself and what's socially acceptable, are very clearly explained as to why they exist and what function they serve.

Although the rules of the game may be clear, the social expectations can be more ambiguous. Here is an intersection between communication and social skills in the context of games and group activities with others. A person on the spectrum will have to adapt to many informal rules such as specific phrases, gestures, facial and body language reactions specific to the game. Just as with conversations where you have invitations and inspirations, group activities are also about throwing the ball back at others in the literal sense. Playing and having fun should not be at the expense of others, they should be invited to participate and be given a fair chance of playing on par with others. If you manage to win it shouldn't result in mocking or excessively teasing comments that hurt the feelings of others. After all, the point is not only to give them an opportunity to participate but with your actions to let everybody feel included, appreciated, and motivated to participate.

The biggest obstacle when it comes to recreational activities is dealing with the competitive element of the game or sport. Somebody will inevitably win, and others will lose, if the teen with ASD happens to be on the losing side, they may get crestfallen and have an excessively negative reaction due to struggles with emotional regulation. It's important to supervise their performance at least in the beginning before the parent or caretaker is certain that the community in which they are has enough trustworthy trainers, figures of authority, and peers who can offer emotional support. As with other areas in life, its important to constantly encourage the child to compare themselves only with their previous performance and realize the progress they've made and to point out that games shouldn't be taken that seriously because there are other considerations, such as the fun they had on the way or the sense of community they were building, which are also hugely important.

Unconventional Ways To Develop Recreational Skills In The Modern Age

For those on the spectrum with more severe spectrums or those suffering from severe social anxiety and inability to engage with other people, it may be better to seek communities and activities where the number of people is reduced, the aim of the activity is less competitive, and they are surrounded by people who they know very well and deeply trust. Going cycling with friends, fishing with your father, or hiking with the whole family are all non-competitive alternatives you can consider if you want activities that are centered more on the fulfillment from the experience itself. Such friendly and more closed environments can also serve as a more smooth transition towards a hobby or a sport that a child wishes to try. If they want to try swimming but happen to be anxious, then they can go with their parents a few times or have a few personal sessions with a trusted coach before progressing to regular training in groups.

If even that's not an option in the present, then two other alternatives can be considered. Keep in mind, that an inability to develop conventional recreational skills now shouldn't lead parents and caregivers to the conclusion that they can't develop recreational skills in the future. In many cases, present hardships, lack of social opportunities, or other time-specific factors can prevent a person from finding success in recreational skills.

The first is to focus on individual hobbies and passions, which can also be very fulfilling and enjoyable. They don't have to be completely asocial as the person can share details on the subject and their experiences with those around them. Furthermore, nowadays, the internet and social media have made it more accessible than ever to join online communities where you can share your experiences and stories and ask for advice from like-minded people who are dedicating themselves to that particular hobby or passion.

A second more modern approach is to encourage your child to join online communities. Many parents tend to stigmatize video games and time spent online as unproductive, unhealthy, or addictive, but it's important to recognize that video games, participation in online communities, or other digital alternatives to recreational activities are not inherently harmful if done in moderation. Playing video games for 12 hours is far from healthy, but helping a person on the spectrum efficiently manage their time and tasks for the day and giving them the opportunity to play video games with friends can be not only a great reward but also a powerful bonding activity.

The unique strength of the online world is the way it gives you near-absolute control over the way you interact with others. People can be completely anonymous or partly share details about themselves, they can selectively interact, start and end conversations, and they are given more time to consider what they want to say before replying. The internet is so vast that geographical or other differences don't limit your ability to meet new people, meaning that you can interact, and bond with like-minded people with who you have lots in common or who at least understand what you are going through and treat you with kindness and respect.

All of those unique benefits can bypass many of the challenges people on the spectrum experience when it comes to anxiety, communication issues, and a struggle to connect with others. Whether it's video games, fan communities for movies, shows, and celebrities, or interactive online games like roleplaying, Dungeons & Dragons, or any other kind of interactive online activity, finding communities and having fun online shouldn't be discouraged or stigmatized.

Chapter Eight

Personal Finance Skills

A core part of being successful as an adult is effectively managing your finances as they can directly influence the standard of living and the amount of freedom you have. People on the spectrum may struggle with budgeting and distributing their money, avoiding temptations, and may fall prey to their own impulsivity or the selfish intentions of others who wish to take advantage of them.

As with any other essential skill that's required for a person to be an optimally functioning and independent adult, personal finance is a skill that ought to be taught gradually from the ground up, beginning with the function and purpose of money and finances and ending with the ability for the person to effectively manage their finances as much as possible.

The Gradual Approach to Personal Finance

Understanding finance begins with knowing everything there is to do with money, the necessary arithmetic which happens with every change, the protocols for exchange and differentiation between coins, bills, credit cards, and every other possible way for payment. Being plunged into adulthood means that suddenly a person has to deal with taxes, bills, paying cashiers, bankers, and any other transaction by themselves. Absolute freedom is intoxicating, but without adequate prior experience, it can lead to impulsive or poorly thought out decisions.

People on the spectrum should be gradually introduced to personal finance and self-responsibility over their money. They should be given pocket money for the whole week and advised to distribute it in a way that sustains them for the whole week. It's better if they waste all their money on junk food in two days when they are 15 instead of wasting their first salary on expensive but superficial items they bought impulsively when they are 19. They should also be encouraged to start shopping along with their parents and caregivers so they can learn how to buy what's required and properly evaluate what ought to be bought.

It's preferable if they also have some exposure to credit cards by setting a separate account for them once it's legal so that their behavior with it can be supervised and they can get used to working with those types of finances as well. One final and often neglected aspect of personal finance is the way they store and display money. If a person on the spectrum struggles to understand the importance of money or fails to recognize the way it may influence others, they may flaunt their money, make poorly thought out comments on how much they own and have, or not protect their wallet adequately which can invite people with immoral intentions to take advantage of that.

How To Independently Manage Finances

A perfect finance system is one where everything is organized to maximize clarity and the efficiency with which you can distribute your income while also automating as many decisions as possible to avoid feeling overwhelmed and to prevent impulsive decisions from threatening your essential expenses.

In much the same way as with note-taking, keeping track of your finances can happen in a notebook, in a digital application for note-taking, or you can rely on personal finance apps like Mint, Stash, etc. The point is for all your flows of income and all your expenses, such as rent, essentials, subscriptions, long-term savings, and money going for emergency funds, to all be categorized so it's clear where your expenses are going and to what extent. For some using an application makes the process very convenient, others prefer relying on their own style and creating huge sheets in Excel or Google Sheets to keep track of everything.

The strength of such a system is not only the clarity that it provides but also the ability for you to consider long-term planning when distributing your finances. Whether it's for a new computer, a course in animation you want to buy, or a vacation and road trip you want to save for, long-term considerations can often escape your thoughts which is where such systems truly shine. There's no single best working system; the point is to find something and experiment with it until it fits your needs which would often involve: ease of use, sustainability of maintaining the system, and actual effectiveness in helping you make better financial decisions.

Even with the most efficient system in place, many people on the spectrum and their caregivers report impulsivity as the biggest cause for concern related to their financial situation. Spontaneous purchases that use most of the person's salary on video games and an expensive electronic reader or anything else that caught their attention are all very common. It's not that people with ASD are irrational and incapable of thinking for themselves, rather, issues with executive function make the stimulation from the purchase much more enticing, and they can't properly self-regulate themselves. The thought of whether this is a good purchase or not is still there, it just doesn't appear faster than the often uncontrollable impulse to make a purchase.

Impulse purchases can not only happen because of that, but society itself heavily leans towards consumerism. Credit cards with no limits where you don't see how much you've given and how much you owe, being constantly exposed to an abundance of items that are all presented in their most attractive angles, and the endless exposure to advertisements that are specifically designed to take advantage of your anxiety, insecurities, and desires all contribute towards even more impulsive purchases.

The solution is not to limit purchases on items and services you want altogether, rather, it should happen in moderation once all other essential and major expenses have been paid for. The most effective solution is to prevent yourself from making most of the impulse purchases that you'd otherwise make. You can easily set up your incomes and bank accounts to automatically lock in part of your finances towards the essential expenses that you have for the month. It's not that the system can't be reserved and you can't eventually draw money from there, but it would take time which allows for you to re-consider whether the purchase you wanted to make really is essential. Another way you can toy with financial accounts is to have a separate category that's entirely for impulsive and miscellaneous purchases, which allows you to intentionally make purchases that excite you rather than having pent-up impulses until you can't wait any longer.

Both the system through which you can track your finances and the way you selectively restrain your impulses by allocating funds automatically to certain accounts rely on the belief in scarcity. Using money is problematic because you have a finite amount of it, and you must make the best possible purchases to maximize the value you get out of the money. Relying excessively on credit cards and allowing yourself to go into debt breaks the whole system because you don't have any restraint, or at least the restraint which comes from the inability to pay off the debt is not one you'd immediately consider when on the verge of making an impulse purchase. This is why using such instantaneous financial tools can have its drawbacks and should be significantly limited.

There are a few more ways to consider if you want to fight impulsivity and win the battle for a proper financial condition. The first is to be intentional in your purchases by evaluating what you need the most and saving money with the intention to buy that. For example, trying to save up for a laptop is hard when the thought of having to buy one was just a whim in your mind two weeks ago, and you sidetracked with all kinds of other purchases from that point onward. Being intentional and planning ahead can even be applicable in your daily life, going shopping is much easier when you don't have to think about what has to be bought on the spot, but instead, you have a prepared list that you are relying upon.

The next strategy you can consider is limiting the temptation that coerces you to make a purchase. Before this strategy is employed, it's important for a person with ASD to receive an explanation of all the various ways in which retail, advertisements, and anybody who sells anything is constantly trying to make them purchase something, which means their intentions are rather selfish and their promises are either false or heavily exaggerated. If it's possible, you should avoid advertisements and certain temptations altogether. If you are constantly on social media and the internet, then there are advertisement-blocking plugins that can be downloaded. If it's feasible, then you can order groceries from your home to avoid the temptation you may experience in the supermarket altogether.

One final strategy to consider is having somebody keep your finances on your behalf or at least assist you with their management. The person could be a parent, close friend, relative, or your partner, anybody for whom you have a lot of trust and belief that they have your best interest in mind. With them, you can discuss purchases before making them to see if they are rational and make sense, they can keep you accountable and make you reflect on the purchases you've made throughout the month to see if they were worth it, and they can restrict the amount of money you have to make sure impulsive purchases are also curbed.

Dealing With Financial Scams and Lucrative Deals

One often neglected aspect of personal finance is the massive proliferation of financial scams, shady salesman, or any other scenario or event in which somebody is trying to steal your money. Financial scams are rapidly becoming more sophisticated and advanced to the point where you can barely distinguish them from legitimate offers. The problem is clear, you could have the best budgeting system and responsibly distribute your finances but one mistake can wipe out your finances and return you to point zero.

Usually, such scams involve somebody pretending to be a representative of a wealthy family, some famous business, or even the banking institution you are using. If they are asking for personal information, such as your name and bank account number, then it's most likely a scam. Very often, those schemes involve asking small transfers out of you or trivial favors for you to deliver or transfer money to someone, and it always includes huge financial rewards in a short amount of time.

More elaborate scams, such as Ponzi schemes, involve agents through emails or targeted advertisements on social media trying to sell you a product or service with the promise of huge returns. This can involve a special and exclusive workshop, finance course, secret strategies and trade secrets that can be used to increase your wealth. With the rise of the stock market and cryptocurrency involvement by regular folks, the amount of such schemes has only grown larger. Such scams rely on fabricated stories of personal success, unrealistic promises for results, limited time offers that create a sense of urgency and an initial "free" part of the product or service as a way to attract you to buy the rest.

Although there may be ways to massively increase your finances through strategic investments at the right time, timing the market is very tricky even for experts and very often it comes down to luck. This is why it's preferable to teach those on the spectrum to be wary and dismissive towards such offers altogether by explaining to them why the promises are unrealistic, making them question the intentions of the offers and showing them how the design is done specifically in a way to manipulate them. In short, if it sounds too good to be true, then it's probably not true.

Chapter Nine

Occupational skills

The ultimate proof of independence is when you begin to earn your income and sustain yourself through employment. For many people, employment is not their primary source of income, but the work they do defines how they feel throughout the day, and their career and the achievements associated with it are a source of pride and accomplishment.

People with ASD are often falsely dismissed as "disabled" and a "burden" because many employers have a narrow and prejudiced look only at the label of their condition instead of recognizing each person on the spectrum as an intelligent individual full of talent and potential. To prove the doubts of many wrong and find professional success, those on the spectrum must find early working opportunities, figure out what they want to do for work, and develop valuable occupational skills.

The Importance of Early Working Experience

Starting a job can feel like entering a whole new world altogether, it's often overwhelming and hard to adapt to the sudden change of routine. Prior working experience can be a blessing as it smoothens out the learning curve because many skills required for work happen to overlap despite the end goal being different.

Schools often have life or social skills programs, local community centers provide internships, and classes on specific niches like cooking are often offered on a local level all throughout the year. Volunteering for various causes is usually available year-round and allows you to meet people of similar interests and personalities while also developing valuable skills.

Managing your time well, following instructions, getting used to a new schedule, and talking with strangers and co-workers are just some of the many essential skills that adolescents with ASD can develop while trying to work from an earlier age. The benefits of early working experience don't just end with the skills that you directly develop. Having prior experience can be a deal-breaker between you and other candidates, and the connections you build at work and in the surrounding communities can get you referrals, letters of recommendation, and other tools through which to strike a future employment opportunity.

Early working experience serves as a signal to future employers that you are a person who's willing to learn and take the initiative to become better, which is what everybody values the most at the end of the day, its not about the starting point of a person but how far they've reached or are willing to push past that point.

One last overlooked benefit of early working experience is the way in which it can change your outlook on life. Very often, choosing where you want to go and where you want to study happens in a bubble, detached from the real world and with no direct experience of how real people interact and how the economy runs. Early working experiences bridge that gap by giving you a direct taste of what various jobs entail in terms of working hours, intensity, expectations, and skills required.

How To Pick The Right Profession

Choosing the right profession for you is one of the most important decisions that people who are about to enter adult-hood ought to consider. Contrary to the way it's presented in current discourse, there's no singular right answer, nor should the decision you make once be the final one since the right profession is one that changes as people change or as they better understand who they are and what they want out of life. Nevertheless, the right profession at the current point in time can be picked if you consider the following factors.

The first factor when choosing a career is to have an end goal in mind. What your end goal is will depend on the way it's phrased, dream, vision, purpose, passion, meaning, or any-thing you want to call it. Each of those has a slightly different meaning, but the overall idea is that you should do something that allows you to positively and meaningfully influence the world while bringing you fulfillment and a sense of purpose while doing so. Choosing where you will study and what you want to work becomes much easier once you have a north star pointing you in the right direction.

The second factor to consider is to think of which professions and careers are compatible with who you are. You have specific personality traits, strengths, and weaknesses that would make some jobs easier and more enjoyable and vice versa. For example, if you are a person who craves consistency and routine, you are better off working a regular 9/5 instead of doing freelance work where employment is uncertain and you have to be constantly hunting down clients. If you struggle with sensory overload, then you better avoid environments in which you will inevitably face unpleasant smells, textures, and noises that make you feel overwhelmed and anxious. If you have excellent long-term memory and are very intelligent, then you may decide to become an architect or an engineer as opposed to becoming a writer because you may struggle with metaphors and idiomatic language in general.

Knowing yourself well enough is the first step, but you should also know whether the degree or professional you wish to pursue can actually be compatible with your preferences, strengths, and interests. Research is required to see what the degree and career you are looking to build looks like, how extensive and hard the educational path is, what are the working conditions like and, what can you expect a usual day to consist of, what is the average salary and in what kind of working day are you expected to have, etc. The internet is a powerful tool that you can use to your advantage because, unlike before, when you had to rely on personal anecdotes from friends and relatives, now you can get the perspective of experts who've studied in a specific university and have been working your desired profession for years. Whether in forums or in video format, the internet is packed with useful insights from people who've personally gone through what you may potentially pursue, and they are willing to share their knowledge.

While research will give you an in-depth understanding of what the degree and profession in general entails, the final decision comes down to you following your gut and choosing what feels right for you. To make the right decision for yourself, you must first overcome any anxiety, low confidence, and doubts you have about your competence. Those feelings are irrational and have no basis in reality, even if you face some challenges and hardships that others don't, that doesn't mean you won't be able to overcome them and reach the same or even greater level of accomplishment compared to neurotypical people.

Finally, throughout this book, we talked about the need to control your impulses and hunches to make decisions on the spot but making a decision based on your gut feeling is fundamentally different. It's not a decision you take in an instant, rather, it's the need to follow your heart's desire after carefully considering most pros, cons, and perspectives on the matter.

Developing Occupational Skills

Occupational skills fall into two categories, those you can learn by yourself and those that can only be acquired at work or in similar environments. In the first category, you can acquire specific skills for a career by enrolling in university or when opting for shorter educational courses on the subject matter.

The internet has truly revolutionized the way in which information is shared, and there has been a massive rise of online courses and educational academics, which offer the ability for people to self-teach themselves in various fields. Learning how to code by yourself or taking a course on nutrition has now become more accessible than ever. Self-initiative and a willingness to experiment and acquire new skills by yourself is a trait that's very often appreciated by employers as it shows the willingness of people to increase their value in the market.

The second type of occupational skills are those that you can develop directly at work or in a similarly challenging environment. Some of those include: being on time for work, managing your time efficiently throughout the day, organizing yourself in a productive way, being able to make the correct decisions quickly through the usage of available information and critical thinking, being able to work in a team, to easily communicate with others and clearly present ideas. You can probably notice that many of those skills overlap with ones we've already discussed previously in the book because many times being productive and living well in your personal life also means you develop habits and systems of organization that can also make you productive at work as well.

Being on time for work can be ensured when you rely on alarms, and reminders, have clocks around your home to make sure that you don't lose track of time, and go out 10-15 minutes earlier just in case. Managing time productively at work means that you have yourself organized, the to-do list, goals, and responsibilities for the day are very clear, which makes the task less overwhelming and easier to start. Clarity can further be enhanced once you make sure to have explicit and straightforward instructions on how to handle the current tasks and project if possible, write down notes when it gets described in meetings, or request a written version of the instructions to keep with you at all times. Planning your work for the day should happen prior to starting work, and you should optimally take a few minutes every day to figure out what your priorities are for the day. Once every few days or once a week, you can do the same but for long-term planning of upcoming projects at work.

It's preferable for work to be done based on your current priorities so that you finish the most important and urgent tasks first before diving into the smaller and more trivial ones later on. For big projects and assignments, you can try to break them up into smaller milestones and goals so that it's easier to navigate and start with the project. When it comes to small assignments, they should not be your biggest priority, but if it's possible to complete something for 2-5 minutes then in between other assignments or when you don't have anything pressing, then it's preferable to do that. Think of all the documents and paperwork that ought to stay organized at work; it doesn't become a chaotic mess at once, rather, it's through continuous delays that the clutter becomes unbearable.

As most of this advice implies, routine is key for productivity. Doing a specific task every single day not only makes you more efficient in the work itself, but it's easier to start and avoid procrastination once the task has become second nature. Not only is getting into a state of flow with the task easier but building a routine of similar tasks and habits one after the other reinforces all of them and makes the transition much more smooth. There is a false and dangerous myth that those with ASD who crave routine can't survive in the modern workplace, which is very dynamic and requires a great amount of flexibility.

Not only is the requirement for flexibility greatly exaggerated and misleading since the description is applicable only for some jobs, but it also falsely portrays this trait as being negative. In reality, being able to consistently come to work and stick with a routine while being hyper-focused on a task is the most effective way to produce value for a company and ultimately find professional and personal success.

While some skills will always be specific to the job you are working on, there are many universal ones like time management, organization, and an ability to follow instructions which are valued everywhere and can be learned and mastered in your personal life as well.

Conclusion

A utism Spectrum Disorder is a condition that manifests in various degrees across people, but no matter the specific circumstances, it likely has a significant impact on a person's life. The irreversible brain differences are often accompanied by other conditions and by secondary challenges in the form of prejudice, stigmatization, and dismissal from peers, communities, and society as a whole. With so many personal hardships and negativity swirling around the label, it's easy to feel discouraged as a parent and caregiver and to start to believe that the situation can't get better. When progress seems out of reach, you may begin to think that one way or another, your child will have to always remain by your side so that nothing exposes them to harm.

Fortunately, the reality is much different than the gloom through which you may be used to viewing the situation. ASD can play a significant influence on the development of a person, but they exist separate from the condition as unique, capable, and powerful individuals who have their own strengths, passions, and interests, which span far beyond the label that society would like to plaster upon them. Just because people on the spectrum have a different starting point in certain areas and struggle with skills that to others are intuitive does not mean they are incapable of significant progress if they put in the consistent effort and dedication towards improvement.

The Importance of Independence

People have a nearly universal desire for autonomy, to feel as though they can independently influence the world around them and sustain themselves. Adolescence is a period full of emotional turbulence where teens begin to piece together the puzzle of who they are and what they want out of life. They grow physically, mentally, and along with everything else, the desire for independence grows even stronger. Being entirely dependent on somebody else can be done with the best intentions, but it's not a sustainable model of living for both parties. Unfortunately, in many cases, it's exhausting and even suffocating as the desire for freedom is one that calls on both children and parents to have some distance in their lives.

Achieving independence is an ambiguous goal since it sets an expectation for constant progress until, at one point, a person is suddenly "independent." In reality, depending on the severity of the condition, a person with ASD will be able to experience different degrees of independence and autonomy. Some maybe learn to function completely on their own, while others may need assistance and support during social events or with the maintenance of a healthy financial situation. Independence not only has different degrees depending upon the personal circumstances of an individual, but it's also not a linear path toward the desired result.

If you think of independence as a bar that can be filled to 100%, then there's no guarantee that every week you will be able to up the percentage, in particularly tense periods where hardships are especially challenging, the bar may even get lower. What matters is that parents and the child retain an unwavering dedication and belief toward a better future, even if the bar doesn't move now, over time, it will eventually given enough effort. Finally, it's important to recognize that there is no deadline until which you ought to fill the bar to 100%, the quest for independence begins in adolescence but it's a lifelong journey of trial and error in which you learn and grow as a person.

Everything Is About Practice

People on the spectrum have an irreversible change in the way their brain is structured and works, but that doesn't mean there is something wrong with them, rather, the world is centered around the way neurotypical people function, and thus there's a need to adapt. Throughout our own journey as parents of a wonderful boy with ASD, we've learned that practice may not make perfect, but it can still lead to significant progress in bridging that gap. You never know just how much better you can become unless you try and give your best.

All the skills we've discussed throughout the book are not only important on their own, but each of them is deeply interconnected with the rest. Personal care is the pillar upon which all other skills rely; social skills are what determine the ability to communicate effectively and engage in recreational activities with others, self-regulation is vital on its own while also improving your personal finance and occupational skills on the way.

While each of those chapters may feel as though it describes an entirely different beast that ought to be tackled, in reality, each skill is interwoven with the rest and makes learning the rest much easier. Improvement in some if not all areas is far from an easy task, progress may not be present in the beginning, and there may be periods of stagnancy or decline, but persevering through everything will eventually lead to significant results. Shooting for the stars isn't about reaching them but about setting a goal and getting as close as possible to it.

As parents and caregivers, you know best which skills must most urgently be taught to your child and you can prioritize them accordingly. Each one should be approached with patience and taken one at a time, trying to learn everything at once even if skills are interconnected is counter-productive and will only leave the child anxious and overwhelmed. All throughout this wonderful and sometimes turbulent journey teens should receive personal and professional support and guidance, motivation when they need it and be nudged to keep trying even in moments of doubt and despair.

Life may be a race but it's not a race with others, rather, it's a tournament where you are only competing with your past self to be a tiny bit better every single day. You've got all the tools you could ever need, it's time for the race to begin.

Thank you so much for reading this book. I hope you found it informative. If you did, please leave a genuine review on Amazon. This way, others can benefit from it as well.

References

1. Grandin, Temple, and Debra Moore. Navigating Autism: 9 Mindsets for Helping Kids on the Spectrum. W.W. Norton &; Company, 2021.

2. Wendler, Daniel. Improve Your Social Skills. Daniel Wendler, 2020.

3. Beardon;Luke. Autism and Asperger Syndrome in Adults, Luke Beardon, 2017.

4. Lau-Zhu, Alex, et al. "Overlaps and Distinctions between Attention Deficit/Hyperactivity Disorder and Autism Spectrum Disorder in Young Adulthood: Systematic Review and Guiding Framework for EEG-Imaging Research." Neuroscience and Biobehavioral Reviews, Pergamon Press, Jan. 2019, https://www.ncbi.nlm.nih.gov/pmc/articles/PMC6331660/.

5. Demetriou, Eleni A, et al. "Executive Function in Autism Spectrum Disorder: History, Theoretical Models, Empirical Findings, and Potential as an En-

dophenotype." Frontiers in Psychiatry, Frontiers Media S.A., 11 Nov. 2019, https://www.ncbi.nlm.nih.gov/pmc/articles/PMC6859507/.